The Mean Girl Motive
Negotiating Power and Femininity

Nicole E.R. Landry

Fernwood Publishing • Halifax & Winnipeg

Editing: Brenda Conroy
Cover Art: John van der Woude
Printed and bound in Canada by Hignell Book Printing

Published in Canada by Fernwood Publishing
Site 2A, Box 5, 32 Oceanvista Lane
Black Point, Nova Scotia, B0J 1B0
and #8 - 222 Osborne Street, Winnipeg, Manitoba, R3L 1Z3
www.fernwoodpublishing.ca

Fernwood Publishing Company Limited gratefully acknowledges the financial support
of the Government of Canada through the Book Publishing Industry Development
Program (BPDIP), the Canada Council for the Arts and the Nova Scotia
Department of Tourism and Culture for our publishing program.

Library and Archives Canada Cataloguing in Publication

Landry, Nicole E. R.
The mean girl motive: negotiating power and femininity / Nicole E.R. Landry.

Includes bibliographical references.
ISBN 978-1-55266-266-3

1. Girls--Psychology. 2. Girls--Social conditions. 3. Aggressiveness in
children. 4. Interpersonal conflict in children. I. Title.

HQ1206.L36 2008   305.23082   C2007-907023-X

Contents

With great thanks and appreciation
to my mentor and friend, Dr. Sandra J. Bell

Acknowledgements

First and foremost, I am indebted to the girls who participated in my research for they were the heart of this project. With little hesitation, they invited me into their world, candidly sharing their stories and revealing their truths about girlhood. As a researcher, I was privileged to be given such an opportunity, one that has greatly impacted my life. I would also like to thank the organization at which I conducted my research for allowing me to talk with their girls. I am especially appreciative of their welcoming nature in light of the hoops that other institutions expect researchers to jump through.

The woman to whom this book is dedicated, Sandra J. Bell, played an integral role in this project; sharing in its excitement, humour, frustration and emotion. The completion of this project is due in large part to her guidance, patience and support.

My sincerest thank you to the staff at Fernwood Publishing, and Errol Sharpe in particular, for not only making this book possible but also recognizing the importance of girl-centred research. I would also like to acknowledge the Social Sciences and Humanities Research Council of Canada for its funding of this project.

Finally, I want to thank my friends and family, whose enthusiasm and encouragement helped motivate me in the completion of this project. My mom and dad, while varied in their roles, have always nurtured my thirst for knowledge. Thus, much of my accomplishments I share in part with them. To Ian, I wish to express my deepest appreciation, as his unyielding love and support keeps me grounded.

Preface

Of the many feminine personas found in mainstream culture today, one of the most misunderstood and devalued is the "mean girl." In Hollywood movies and bestselling books, the topic of meanness has experienced vast exposure and perked public interest. While our fascination with the mean girl has succeeded in bringing girl culture into the limelight, it has also generated many negative repercussions in regards to the ways in which girl-centred issues are defined and addressed. Indeed, the ever-expanding crusade against bullying has adopted meanness as its most recent issue, with girls being condemned as the worst kind of bullies.

My interest in the topic of "girl bullying" developed from my work as a criminology student at Saint Mary's University in the area of youth justice. After emerging myself in the "bullying" literature, I uncovered a trend that was particularly alarming. Prior to the 1980s, girls were completely excluded from research on childhood aggression, presumably because their feminine natures made them adverse to aggression. Yet, very disturbing is the way in which this blatant omission of girls is being addressed in the academic literature and public discourse, as well as in mainstream culture. The once non-existent issue of "aggressive girls" has transformed into an epidemic of grand proportions, one that has suffered grave ignorance at the hands of adult proprietors. Not only were girls missing from earlier research, their voices are frequently absent in the current "girl aggression" discourse. Despite this, the problem with mean girls has received growing attention, especially in the field of psychology. However, besides the incessant conclusions that boys and girls aggress differently, much of this work has only offered a means of readily labelling, identifying and thus further problematizing girls' so-called mean behaviour.

Moving beyond the superficial, this book explores the social context of girls' mean behaviour, examining the intersection between structures of class, race and gender in the production of girls' aggression. Drawing on girls' first-hand knowledge and experiences, this study provides a candid glimpse into girl culture that raises critical questions about our "taken for granted knowledge" of girls' meanness.

Where Have All the Good Girls Gone?

Through recent media depictions of youth crime, it would appear as though adolescent girls are no longer made of "sugar and spice and everything nice," as the childhood nursery rhyme once suggested. Indeed, it no doubt comes as a great shock to the public to read of "bad girls," who have seemingly become as aggressive and violent as boys. This view is furthered by ever-emerging "experts" on the subject of girl behaviour, such as James Garbarino, who has capitalized on this topic by publishing an anti-girl book entitled *See Jane Hit.*

In relation to this growing concern over aggressive girls, Chesney-Lind and Pasko maintain that the "bad girl" discourse can be divided into two eras. The first, in the early 1990s, revolved around girls, particularly girls of colour, who engaged in what has been traditionally perceived as masculine behaviour, namely gang membership, weapon possession and violent alterca-tions. Toward the end of the 1990s, the focus shifted away from gun-toting gang girls and onto white girls, whose aggression is characterized as meanness (Chesney-Lind and Pasko 2004: 31). In both scenarios, the message being conveyed to the public is that girls' aggression is not to be taken lightly.

Since the murder of fourteen-year-old Reena Virk in 1997, involving a group of seven teenaged girls and one boy in British Columbia, the media has become fixated on an apparent rise in girl violence. In 2000, a four-teen-year-old girl, Dawne-Marie Wesley, hung herself after allegedly being bullied by three girls at her school. She left behind a suicide note claiming that she could not take their abuse any longer. The media uses these isolated incidents, publishing a series of stories that highlight the same case over and over, and thereby fueling a public panic concerning the "new" problem of girl violence.

Notwithstanding the media's propensity to sensationalize an issue, public panics are heightened with the release of statistics that seemingly support perceived increases in violent crimes committed by girls (Schissel 1997). Nevertheless, it is important to recognize, as Adler and Worrall point out, that "statistics are as much an indication of definitions of particular behaviors, and the criminal or juvenile justice system responses to them and to particular individuals, as they are about the actions of young women" (2004: 5). The question of whether there is a "real" or merely perceived rise in girl violence is muddied by the fact that our knowledge of girls' aggression is limited. It is illogical to speculate about changes in girls' behaviour when we have only just recently begun to study aggressive behaviour among girls.

The first chapter in this book opens with a discussion of the literature on girl aggression to both familiarize the reader with the topic as well as highlight the theoretical, epistemological and methodology issues arising from this work. Particularly problematic in much of the literature are the psychologically oriented explanations of girls' so-called meanness and a failure to acknowledge factors beyond the individual. My work draws primarily on feminist analysis, which provides a framework from which to understand female aggression in terms of girls' inferior status in society; feminist research examines aspects of power, femininity, patriarchy and structures of gender, race and class, which are virtually ignored in most of academic research on girl aggression.

The second chapter examines the development of the theoretical framework I used to analyze and interpret "class" in the context of girlhood. This chapter begins with an examination of Marxian class theory, which is critiqued by feminists for its disregard of gender relations. Equally problematic is the exclusion of youth and, more specifically to my research, girls in a Marxist analysis of social class. Drawing on feminist theory, I provide a theoretical framework that is relevant to girl studies because it conceptualizes class as a cultural identity derived from an analysis of femininity. The discussion in this chapter raises a number of research questions: Do girls of minority or marginalized positions feel less constrained to hide their aggression than girls who occupy a higher status? Do girls associate power with physical force? What does power represent for girls? How do girls' lessons in aggression compare along race and class categories? And is femininity negotiated for girls who are involved in overt forms of aggression or violence, and if so, how is it negotiated?

Chapter three outlines the methodologies I employed to answer these questions. I conducted focus groups with girls aged eight to eleven and adopted a feminist qualitative research methodology that draws on girls' lived experiences of aggression and class. My findings are discussed in chapters four and five, where I highlight important links between structures of power, gender, class and race in relation to the mean girl epidemic. My final chapter provides an analysis of key findings as well as a discussion of the theoretical, methodological and epistemological contributions from this research. More importantly, chapter six outlines some implications that my research has on what we think we know about girls' aggression.

Chapter One

Girl Aggression

This chapter highlights the research that has been done on girl aggression, beginning with early work that first identified gender differences in relation to childhood aggression. In recent years, research on girl aggression has dispersed in many directions. I am particularly interested in studies that examine the social contexts of girls' aggression, i.e., popularity/peer status, patriarchy, femininity and race/ethnicity. The bulk of this chapter discusses these social structures and how they are thought to influence girls' aggression.

"Discovering" Aggression in Girls

Largely due to the widespread belief that aggression was a male phenomenon, studies prior to the 1980s focused specifically on the behaviour of young boys (Buss 1961; Maccoby and Jacklin 1974; Olweus 1978). One of the first groups to study girls' aggression in any depth was the Finnish research team of Björkqvist, Lagerspetz and Kaukiainen in 1992. They "discovered" that girls are not completely averse to aggression but, rather, participate in this type of behaviour in a more covert manner than boys. Other academics, such as Crick and Grotpeter (1995) and Tomada and Schneider (1997), conducted research that provided further support for this notion of girls' hidden form of aggression, which has been termed "relational aggression."[11] More recent research on girl aggression, mostly from the field of psychology, examines such things as motives and intentions (Sumrall et al. 2000), regulation of emotions such as anger and jealousy (Smith and Thomas 2000; Prinstein et al. 2001; Conway 2005; Parker et al. 2005), internalizing behaviours such as depression (Casey-Cannon et al. 2001; Barton and Cohen 2004), developmental changes such as social maladjustment (Cillessen and Mayeux 2004), antisocial behaviour (Susman and Pajer 2004; Putallaz et al. 2004; Bierman et al. 2004), cognitive development (Cummings and Leschied 2000 and 2001; Hipwell et al. 2002; Brendgen et al. 2005), normative belief structures (Werner and Nixon 2005), ADHD diagnoses (Zalecki and Hinshaw 2004), reactive and proactive aggression (Camodeca et al. 2002) and self-other representations (Moretti et al. 2001).

While the early work on girl aggression succeeded in bringing girls into academic inquiry, for the most part, the more recent work on relational aggression is focused on cognitive explanations of girls' aggression. Even when these researchers extend their focus beyond individual psychology and attempt to address the social contexts of aggression, they merely focus on family structure. Most commonly, factors such as parental involvement and "maternal psychology" are identified as influential (Carlo et al. 1999; Zahn-Waxler and Polanichka 2004; Loukas et al. 2005). In 2005, Giles and Heyman examined children's beliefs about aggression and gender, concluding that children themselves view social alienation, gossip and slander as "female" problems. The approaches taken by these researchers add little to a sociological examination of the topic.

Meanness and Popularity

Widening the scope of analysis from the individual to the peer group, some recent studies on relational aggression have indicated that this type of covert behaviour is related to girls' popularity and peer status. For instance, in focus groups conducted by Owens, Shute and Slee (2000), girls aged fifteen and sixteen indicated that relational aggression is often used to obtain a popular status within a particular peer group. In isolating popularity as an important component of girls' aggression, Owens et al. suggest that meanness holds a specific purpose among girls. Others, such as Salmivalli, Kaukiainen and Lagerspetz (2000) and Werner and Crick (2004), examined peer status in relation to children's aggression, and, although they did not look at girls exclusively, suggest that peer rejection is positively correlated with aggression levels. Crain, Finch and Foster (2005), who examined social cognitive variables such as social goals and hostile intent attributions in relation to girls' aggression, concluded that relational aggression might be more determined by social contextual factors, such as peer dynamics than social cognition. These later studies have significant implications for my research as they indicate that popularity, as a motive, is an important variable to be examined. Unfortunately, they neglect to analyze how popularity functions in girls' everyday lives or even why or how meanness is linked to popularity. Other literature indicates that girls' meanness and the pursuit of popularity is linked with power.

Popularity and Power

Merton's (1997) study of girls' aggression found that popularity was equated with social power and, thus, he argues that girls use meanness to achieve power (188). Lease, Kennedy and Axelrod (2002) investigated the social construction and meaning of popularity among youth, and they too found that popularity was perceived as an important determinant of social power in peer groups. In addition, they argue that popularity calculations among girls are based on attractiveness and spending power. Phillips (2003) explored the "pecking orders" of youth hierarchies and concluded that relational aggression is a normal function in the lives of girls as it enables them to maintain and enhance their reputations. Rose, Swenson and Walker (2004) claim that perceived popularity is positively correlated with relational aggression in girls. In other words, so-called relational aggression is more common among popular girls. In line with this argument, Cillessen and Mayeux (2004) contend that girls experience social benefits from utilizing relational aggression and, thus, similar to the argument made by Phillips (2003), this behaviour may be perpetuated because it allows girls to maintain or enhance their status among peers.

These works offer a more sociological analysis of girls' aggression, one that explores popularity and power, and they suggest that girls' use of meanness can be understood as a way of exercising power in girl culture. Yet, none of these studies provide an explanation for how and why aggression functions as a means for girls to obtain power. In contrast, feminist writers provide a framework from which to understand the relationship between meanness and power, arguing that patriarchal structures shape the lessons as well as the rules that girls' receive about aggression.

Locating Power in Meanness

In order to understand why girls engage in mean behaviour we need to look at the genderization[22] of aggression. In other words, what do girls learn about aggression? Campbell (1993) contends that "a major impact of gender identity for girls is the suppression of their own aggression. Boys, however, enter a period in which they recognize aggression as an important component of being male" (26). Thus, children receive gendered lessons in aggression: girls learn to avoid using aggression; boys are encouraged to behave in an aggressive manner. Campbell (1993) states: "The most remarkable thing about the socialization of aggression in girls is its absence. Girls do not learn the right way to express aggression, they simply learn not to express it" (20). Gilligan (1993) argues that girls become increasingly aware of the limitations placed on their anger and aggression in adolescence. She refers to this as "a kind of voice and ear training" that outlines what girls can and cannot do or say (Gilligan 1993: 149).

In speaking about women's aggression, Crowley Jack (1999) supports Campbell's argument by claiming that women mask their aggression because of their "childhood training" (191). She found that "most women say they learned to avoid conflict by watching their mothers" (192). Many of the women Crowley Jack interviewed spoke of their mothers' passive-aggressive demeanor. The women indicated that they would play the submissive role in their relationships with men because they did not wish to challenge the power structures that are often assumed and upheld in the family unit. As well, the women reported hiding their frustrations by manipulating their relationships, oftentimes with other women, as a means of achieving some control over their lives (193).

Miller and White (2004) also argue that gender training is an important predictor of girls' aggression. In other words, it is important to examine the contradicting lessons that girls and boys receive concerning aggression. Miller and White contend that "women and men 'do gender' in response to normative beliefs about femininity and masculinity" (168). They maintain that understanding girls' aggression requires an analysis of gender inequalities; it is necessary to examine the ways in which power imbalances between men and women constrain girls' use of aggression (169). In a society that permits and even celebrates male violence, girls' use of aggression must be passively negotiated to ensure that they do not undermine men's power. In an examination of gender role identities and relational aggression, Crothers, Field and Kolbert (2005) draw a similar conclusion, claiming "femininity restricts options for conflict management either to the use of relational aggression or to the suppression of wants and feelings" (353). Ultimately, girls are limited to the use of meanness in addressing conflict or negotiating power because they are expected to uphold feminine norms, such as being nurturing and kind, and are not permitted the use of overt aggression.

Similarly, gender norms constrain girls' negotiations with status and their access to power. Emphasizing this point, Miller and White (2004) argue that an analysis of girl aggression must consider "how young women negotiate within gender-stratified settings, and how they accommodate and adapt to gender inequality in their commission of violence" (170). Therefore, girls' aggression must be examined within the context of gender stratification. In this vein, Artz (1998) suggests that girls' violence is related to their state of powerlessness in society. She argues that aggression, which is usually expressed passively through meanness, becomes a tool whereby teenage girls can gain power, whether it is over a group of girls or one particular girl. Consequently, girls may learn the rules of patriarchy through the dynamics of familial relations — in other words, how power is distributed between the mother and the father. In the lives of the girls in Artz's study, violence and intimidation were prominent tools employed by the father figure to control and discipline but also to maintain the hierarchy within the family (69). Artz (1998) contends that the message conveyed to girls is that "men are far more important and more powerful than women, and that men's importance is not connected to the contributions they make to the greater good. Rather, it is bound up in their being stronger and more forceful than women" (171).

Girls also learn that men use aggression as a means of asserting their power over women. Jiwani (2006) argues that "any hierarchal system sustains itself through the deployment of categories whereby groups can be defined and ranked in terms of their access to varying degrees of power and privilege" (9). Being categorized as both "youth" and "female" locates girls at the bottom of two hierarchal systems defined by ageism and sexism, which position men on top, followed by women, then boys and then girls.

For Brown (2003), a girl's involvement in aggression is not only determined by her social status among her peers but also by her inferior position as female in a patriarchal society. Moreover, Brown argues that "girls' treatment of other girls is too often a reflection of and reaction to the way society sees and treats them" (32). Because girls' power is usually generated through feminine qualities such as their appearance, their innocence and their passivity, they are often forced to compete with one another under these limited criteria. As concludes, "Girls' meanness to other girls is a result of their struggle to make sense of or reject their secondary status in the world and to find ways to have power and to experience feeling powerful" (32).

Occupying a subordinate position in society, girls adopt passive aggressive tactics such as meanness that allow them to negotiate their status among other girls. Brown (2003) argues that patriarchy shames girls into choosing "undetectable ways to police others" (p.107). According to the work of Campbell (1993), Gilligan (1993), Artz (1998), Crowley Jack (1999), Brown (2003), Miller and White (2004) and Jiwani (2006), girls' gender training and policing prohibit them from engaging in aggressive negotiations of power, and, thus, they are forced to develop alternate and more covert tactics of achieving a sense of power or status.

The Feminine Hierarchy

Expanding on notions of girls' power, Currie and Kelly (2006) argue that while girls lack economic and political power in the school, the one kind of power they do possess is the ability to establish hierarchies between groups of girls (158). In addition, they contend that girls' meanness places girls in a "gendered economy" where "the currency is being pretty, being skinny and behaving in ways that win male attention" (163). Brown (2003) contends that "there is one acceptable avenue to power: be nice, stay pure, look beautiful, act white, be chosen" (21). In her study of the prom and youth culture, Best (2000) found that feminine spaces are sites upon which "girls have some measure of power and control (though limited)" (93). In addition, Best (2000) argues that "the system through which popularity gains currency is bound to normative constructions of masculinity and femininity; typically the most popular girls are also viewed as the most feminine girls" (72). In other words, femininity is powerful social capital for girls. Furthermore, in line with Currie and Kelly, Best (2000) contends that "girls' popularity is based principally upon standards of attractiveness" (72). As a result, girls can locate power through an evaluation of other girls' femininity.

For girls, gaining power is not simply a matter of spreading gossip and thereby becoming popular; it is highly influenced by structures of patriarchy. As Best argues, "It is men's assessment of women's attractiveness that chiefly determines women's location within this status system" (72). Moreover, Currie and Kelly (2006), drawing on the work of Hey (1997), contend that "meanness regulates membership in the prized clique of womanhood by controlling (or attempting to control) claim to these resources; as a consequence it polices the boundaries of idealized femininity through the surveillance by the male gaze" (163). Male admirers gauge the value of girls' femininity. As well, Jiwani (2006) argues that "particular notions of what is considered beauty and, what an ideal type body should look like are also assessed in terms of whether these bodies can and do attract the attention of boys and young men" (76). Hence, while femininity is a resource for girls' agency and power, it also authorizes "girls as objects rather than subjects of desire" (Currie and Kelly 2006: 169). Moreover, Fine (1997), cited by Currie and Kelly (2006), contends that young women may be encouraged to be sexually desirable, yet, "they are negatively sanctioned for expressing sexual agency" (169), thereby ensuring that girls' access to power is heavily dependent on male reinforcement and approval of their sexuality and femininity.

From her work on girls' aggression, Simmons (2002) would argue that the valued qualities of femininity, being nice and beautiful, are instilled in the daughters of middle-class society. Lending support to her claim, Currie and Kelly (2006) contend that these feminine traits are "tenets of middle-class femininity" (169) and they reinforce the "mandate for niceness" (171). According to Brown (2003), white, middle-class society sets the bar for the dominant ideal of femininity with the expectation that young girls will be nice and caring individuals who grow up to be nice and caring mothers (55). Furthering this argument concerning class-specific femininity, Jiwani (2006) maintains that feminine standards are not only reflective of gendered and classed identities but they are also racialized. In particular, Jiwani (2006) suggests, "whiteness carries with it connotations of slimness, beauty, sexuality and a certain look" and this idealization of "whiteness" is particularly complex for racialized girls (76).

According to Chesney-Lind and Shelden (1998) it is difficult for minority and/or girls from working-class backgrounds to achieve a popular status when popularity is centred around white, middle-class standards of beauty. Chesney-Lind and Brown (1999) contend that girls' and women's socialization is greatly influenced by culture, race and social class, while Flannery and Huff (1999) note that, "expectations about what constitutes appropriate behavior vary by class" (173).

In studying girl gangs and femininity, Laidler and Hunt (2001) claim that girls of lower- and working-class backgrounds negotiate femininity differently from middle- and upper-class girls. Drawing from the work of Messerschmidt (1997), Laidler and Hunt (2001) propose that girl gang members create "alternative forms of femininity," referred to as "bad girl" femininity: defined by independence, respect and reputations (675). Working-class girls, given their socio-economic position, use their sense of independence to maintain a particular reputation and gain respect from their peers. Seemingly, "bad girl" femininity provides a survival mechanism for girls whose social settings may not reward niceness to the same extent as middle-class society. Laidler and Hunt (2001) claim that femininity is constantly being negotiated in accordance with a girl's social circumstance; thus, notions of femininity are never fixed. They contend, "These interactions and negotiated definitions of femininity occur within the race, class and patriarchal constraints of a larger social structure. Young women's location within the social structure simultaneously affects their interactions and their notions of being feminine" (Laidler and Hunt 2001: 660).

While structures of patriarchy may force some girls to invent alternate ways of exhibiting their aggression, there are other social structures, such as race,[33] ethnicity[44] and class, that can affect a girl's femininity and, thus, her access to power. Certainly, this begs a number of questions: Are there different versions of femininity? Do girls who engage in direct forms of aggression reject middle-class ideals of femininity? How do girls' notions of femininity affect how they aggress?

Discourses of Diversity

While a feminist analysis of patriarchy can affectively account for most girls' avoidance of aggression, it does not explain some girls' engagement in physical aggression and violence. Miller and White (2004), suggesting that there is a social context to girls' aggression, argue that "girls' use of violence varies across circumstances, and is shaped by motives and goals, by the gender of the other parties involved, and by the situations in which it occurs" (175). The circumstances of girls' diverse experiences are inevitably shaped by structures of gender as well as class and race. Batacharya (2004) argues that "violence occurs among girls along lines of systemic relations of power — race, class, nationality, language, body size, and appearance, skin color, and disability" (68).

Twenty years ago, Campbell's (1984 and 1990) studies of girls' membership in Hispanic gangs reported that these girls, as members of the urban underclass, are powerless in light of "all the burdens of their triple handicaps of race, class and gender" (1990: 50). More recently, Chesney-Lind and Pasko

(2004) highlight the effects of race, class and gender on girls' participation in gangs and violence and claim that an increase in research on girl gang membership has put some "much-needed attention on the lives of girls of color" (43). They conclude that research on girl gangs must be "sensitive to the contexts within which they arise" (54). According to Jiwani (2006), every aspect of girls' lives is best understood when "positioned at the intersections of race, gender, class, geographic locations, (dis)ability, sexuality, language and cultural heritage" (64). She argues: "Experiences of 'being a girl' are intrinsically tied to the multiplicity of social processes that interact to shape our social contexts and identities" (64).

While gender is an important component of girls' meanness, it is naïve to presume that girls are defined by structures of patriarchy alone. Girls' aggression is not exclusively a gendered phenomenon because not all girls succumb to the pressures of suppressing their aggression. Feminine standards and aggression are contingent on structures of race and class; girls are not necessarily limited to one version of femininity or one form of aggression. Rather, there are girls who express their aggression directly and even in the form of physical violence, while most girls suppress their aggression or channel it into acts of meanness.

The media would lead us to believe that aggression takes various forms in girl culture and its portrayal of girl aggression is also gendered, racialized[55] and classed. Lamb (2001) contends that public reaction to girls' aggression varies considerably depending on a girl's class and racial background. She argues that we tolerate aggression among lower-class girls as their lives are of little concern, while any sign of aggression among middle-class girls is closely monitored and denounced (Lamb 2001: 142). Certainly, this argument suggests the extent to which structures of race and class influence how different "types" of girls are problematized in the media.

Before the "mean girl" epidemic, public discourse was fixated on another so-called villain: the "violent girl," and these images have been associated with racialized versions of girl aggression. Chesney-Lind and Irwin (2004) argue that much of the discourse through the 1990s surrounding girl violence, particularly in the United States, focused exclusively on marginalized and minority girls' behaviour and, more specifically, on African-American and Latino girl gangs (47). They also contend that recently there has been a distinct shift in the public's concern for girls' aggressive behaviour, from the "violent gang girl" to the "mean queen bee" (Chesney-Lind and Irwin 2004: 50). This group is white and middle-class and their meanness and "manipulative behaviours" have now been defined as dangerous aggressive behaviour. Certainly, this "exposure" of the "mean girl" has induced a different level of public fear than did the "violent girl." After all, the violent girls were thought to be identifiable as poverty-stricken racial minorities. On the other hand, mean girls are presented as especially dangerous because they are the hidden and unpredictable aggressor. Thus, not only do media images of the mean girl defy previous racialized portraits of girl aggression but they have also prompted questions about the integrity and genuineness of feminine qualities such as niceness that are supposedly intrinsically female. As stated in an article featured in *Homemakers Magazine* in 1999:

> Once persistent "sugar and spice" cultural stereotypes are dying hard as researchers point to evidence showing that girls have always felt as much anger as boys; they've just been encouraged to channel their aggression in to more socially acceptable "feminine" behaviors — like gossiping, name-calling and excluding the kids they want to punish. Furthermore, these so-called mean girls are assumed to be the daughters of the respectable, middle-class population; a perception that only adds to the perceived threat. (Graydon 1999)

Both popular and scholarly discourse have isolated distinct racial and class differences in relation to girls' aggression. For instance, Lamb (2001) argues that girls who grow up in environments characterized by poverty and racial injustice are taught to wear their aggression with pride as it is thought to be a method of survival and resistance against oppression (141). Chesney-Lind and Joe (1995) claim that for marginalized and minority girls, "fighting and violence is a part of their life in the gang but not something they necessarily seek out. Instead, protection from neighborhood and family violence was a consistent and major theme in the girls' interviews" (cited in Chesney-Lind and Pasko 2004: 51).

Simmons (2002) argues that in cases where a child is growing up under conditions of economic hardship and/or racial oppression, it seems that parents will often teach their child to use aggression as a means of resistance, self-assertion and protection from subordination (185). Furthermore, Simmons (2002) claims that African American girls are awarded a kind of "cultural permission" to express their aggression overtly (188). Taylor, Gilligan and Sullivan (1995) found that African-American girls were not socialized under the same constraints of aggression and anger as white, middle-class girls. From her ethnographic research on girl violence in Philadelphia, Ness (2004) makes the argument that meanness is a middle-class issue, claiming that conflicts surrounding issues of jealousy are settled differently among girls from poor neighbourhoods. Furthermore, she argues that relational aggression is not an alterative to physical aggression, but rather, restrictions against violence are stronger in middle-class culture. Thus, middle-class girls more commonly employ tactics of meanness, while lower-class girls often settle their issues through physical force (Ness 2004: 41).

Conclusion

These arguments present girls' aggression in two opposing forms, relational and physical; they allude to particular classes of girls and they suggest that lower-class girls tend to use overt forms of aggression while middle-class girls engage in meanness. While this raises the important question of whether girls' meanness is a white, middle-class issue, other arguments about middle-class standards of femininity suggest that further questions are important: Are marginalized and minority girls more likely to engage in direct aggression? Should we rely on racialized and classed versions of femininity to predict girls' aggression? Other works that highlight significant class differences in relation to girls' aggression lack a framework from which to define or analyze class in the context of girl culture. Therefore, in order to examine how a girl's class affects how she will aggress, it is first necessary to proceed with a theoretical examination of the concept of social class.

Notes

1. Relational aggression is characterized by behaviors that "inflict harm on others by manipulating their peer relationships," for example, "giving a peer the silent treatment, maliciously spreading lies and rumors about a peer to damage the peer's group status" (Crick and Grotpeter 1995: 711).
2. "Genderization" refers to the processes of assigning socially constructed gender scripts to individuals.
3. The term "race" is a "socially constructed category based on beliefs about biological differences between groups of people that have no basis in scientific evidence" (Bell 2006: 382).
4. "Ethnicity" is a concept that refers to a person's group of origin, where origin is usually thought of in terms of geographical place and/or elements of culture such as language, style of dress, behavioural patterns and social customs (Bell 2006: 378).
5. The term "racialized" is defined as a "concept that allows an understanding of racism that goes beyond overt expressions and discriminatory actions of individuals, referring more to underlying assumptions in discourse and practice" (Bell 2006: 382).

Chapter Two

Defining Class in Girl Culture

Since the class categories to which we have traditionally subscribed are defined by the capitalist economic system, the first section of this chapter explores class theory that is centred on capitalism and production from Marxists and neo-Marxists. While it has made important and significant theoretical contributions to our knowledge of class structures and dynamics, Marxism has been critiqued by feminist writers for its failure to examine the sexual division of labour and structures of patriarchy. Thus, the focus of this section outlines feminist critiques of Marxism. In addition to its disregard for gender relations, Marxist frameworks also ignore youth as well as women. Pertinent to my research is a theoretical understanding of "class" that directly lends itself to girl culture and considers both gender and age. Consequently, the concluding sections of this chapter highlight the work of feminist writers such as Lawler, Reay, Walkerdine, Bettie, Proweller and McRobbie. Their theories on class provide a framework from which to analyze girls' class in terms of hierarchies of femininity.

Capitalism and Production

Although social class is a term frequently used in the disciplines of sociology and criminology alike, it has no universal definition that all academics agree upon.[11] Certainly, this generates some difficulty for researchers conducting class analyses. Indisputably, class theory has its origin in the work of Karl Marx and Friedrich Engels. Messerschmidt (1986) provides a comprehensive overview of Marxian class theory, contending that the key to understanding any capitalist society is to focus on the mode of production; thus, social class develops through individuals' common relations to the means of production and the appropriation of the surplus (2). More specifically, Marx and Engels identified four social classes characteristic of capitalist societies: the bourgeoisie, more commonly known as the capitalists; the petit bourgeoisie, made up of artisans, professionals and entrepreneurs; the proletariat or the working class; and finally, the lumpenproletariat, the impoverished and unemployed (30). Most vital to the capitalist system are the capitalists and the working class: the former own the means of production and capital; the working class sell their labour power to the capitalists. Capitalists accumulate profits by providing a wage that is far less than the value of the product that the working class are producing (31). Ehrenreich (1996) argues that the relationship between these two classes is one of "irreconcilable antagonism" (71) and that this ruling class system is maintained by force. She contends that "only by waging a revolutionary struggle aimed at the seizure of state power can the working class free itself, and, ultimately, all people" (71).

Even today, this conceptualization of social class is viewed as a progressive analysis of capitalism. Indeed, class structures based on employment income remain through class categories such as middle-class or working-class. Thus, this conceptualization of class is relevant in framing a discussion of girls' socio-economic background, which is commonly derived from parents' employment status and income. However, relying entirely on these categories to give meaning to a girl's class is problematic, and feminist theorists, in particular, have identified the limitations of Marxist theories of class.

Marxism has come under fire for neglecting to examine gender relations. In his later work, Engels attempted to rationalize Marx's blatant disregard of women by claiming that the first division of labour occurs in the family and arises spontaneously from the differences between the sexes. Rather than view this sexual division of labour as the subordination of women, Engels argued that it is a "natural" process that results in "men producing the means of subsistence while women work in the household" (Messerschmidt 1986: 3). Because Marxism defines class in terms of one's relationship to the means of production (outside the home), a woman's social class is often contingent on that of her husband's. Commenting on Engels' account of the sexual division of labour, Burstyn (1985) contends, "In locating women's oppression 'out there' in the abstract social relations of a class society rather than in the real relations of masculine control and appropriation of women's labor, Engels renders the sexual division of labor itself as a non-issue and, in strategic terms, essentially unimportant" (25). Clearly, Marxism has ignored structures of patriarchy that have confined women to the home and denied them equal opportunities alongside men in the labour force. The sexual division of labour is not a product of nature but rather the consequence of women's oppression. More importantly for this book, Marxism's focus on capitalism and its failure to acknowledge the constraints of patriarchy on the formation of class structures also limits its ability to analyze class in girl culture.

In opposition to Marxism's disregard of gender, socialist feminists such as Joan Acker (1973) argue that "gender and class inequalities have a mutual influence and cannot be analyzed in isolation from each other" (cited in Abbott and Sapsford 1987: 9). In other words, a theory of class is required that adequately addresses the relationship between patriarchy and capitalism. Acker (1973) summarizes the major feminist rejections of conventional class theory, including Marxism, as follows:

(i) the assumption that the family is the rational unit of analysis, with complete class equivalence with it; (ii) that the social position of the family is determined by the occupation of the head of the household; (iii) that the male is necessarily the head of the household, if such a position has to be distinguished; (iv) that none the less women somehow determine their own class position when they do not happen to be living with an adult male; and (v) that the inequalities between men and women are inherent and inevitable, (cited in Abbott and Sapsford 1987: 3)

While feminist critiques brought women to the forefront of discussions on class, assigning a social class to individual women has remained problematic. Armstrong and Armstrong (1985) maintain that women are still either assigned the same class position as their husbands or are grouped into a category with other women who perform similar domestic duties (24). To complicate matters further, women who are directly involved in the workforce are concentrated in low-wage, lower-status jobs and, even when women achieve a higher income job, they still occupy the "buffer zone" at the bottom of each class. Therefore, a woman's class position cannot be rendered independent of the oppression that she suffers due to the patriarchal nature of a capitalist labour force. Abbott and Sapsford (1987) argue that in a capitalist society there is a mutually influential relationship between women's work inside and outside the home, and this has serious implications for class construction and awareness (14). For this reason, women's experiences of social class differ entirely from those of men, yet these gender differences have been neglected in Marxian class theory.

Feminism and Social Class

Seeking a gender analysis of class structures, I initially turned to socialist feminism in developing a theoretical framework for my research. This seemed the most appropriate framework given the socialist feminists' critique of the "masculine construct of class" and the "sexual division of labor" (Ehrenreich 1976: 71). Furthermore, because this perspective focuses primarily on women and class, its theoretical framework should also be applicable to girls. Indeed, socialist feminists argue that traditional class theories have ignored women, rendering them classless, and this is also the situation with youth and, more specifically, girls. In addition, it has been common practice for women to be placed in the same class category as their husbands, much like youth assignments to the class position of their parents, at least until they have secured full-time employment of their own.

Socialist feminism recognizes the dual importance of examining class and gender and more specifically, how the oppressive structures of patriarchy and capitalism affect women and girls. Ehrenreich (1976) exemplifies this point by stating, "We understand a class as being composed of people, and as having a social existence quite apart from the capitalist-dominated realm of production" (74). This understanding of class is also relevant to girls, as they have yet to enter into the labour force and, thus, have no relationship with the means of production beyond that of their parents.

Once immersed in the feminist literature that discusses women and class, I came to discover that not all feminist theorists who analyze gender and class identify themselves as socialist feminists. While most of the literature discussed in this book falls under the broad category of feminist theory, many feminists, such as Chesney-Lind, Artz, Proweller, Brown, Bettie, Best and McRobbie, also align themselves with the academic disciplines of criminology, education, psychology and cultural studies. Indeed, the compartmentalization of feminism into smaller disciplines such as socialist feminism, feminist criminology and feminist psychology complicates the categorization of feminist research as a whole. In other words, it is not as simple as adopting a specific feminist framework, such as socialist feminism, because there are feminist writers who address class and gender without assuming that label. In an effort to resist labelling, feminist theory is the primary platform upon which I have situated my research. Yet, to directly address my research questions concerning class and girl aggression, it was important to narrow my theoretical framework to those feminist theorists who have specifically addressed class and women through an analysis of femininity, e.g., Walkerdine, Hey, Lawler and Reay, feminists who have identified themselves as "class matters" theorists.

Genderizing Class

Walkerdine et al. (2001) note that "feminist critics have powerfully challenged this privileging of the labour market as the main site in which individuals come to understand themselves as classed subjects" (cited in Hey 2003: 324). Some feminist writers perceive class as more of a "lived experience" than a labour-market label. Hey (2003), for example, contends that "we need a more embodied reading of class and consciousness" (322). She asserts that class-consciousness begins to develop well before one enters the labour force, and therefore, it should be conceptualized in conjunction with the personal, sexual and social in addition to the economic division of labour (324).

Central to feminist critiques of traditional class discussions are narratives surrounding the "end of the working class." Lawler (2005) explains that because of the decline of manufacturing jobs, it has become disagreeable to be working-class, and thus, "This class has now disappeared, to be either absorbed into an allegedly-expanding middle class, or consigned to a workless and workshy underclass which lacks taste, is politically retrogressive, dresses badly, and above all, is prey to a consumer culture" (434).

Another relevant point being made is that the middle-class is supposedly expanding, in that more individuals are aiming to situate themselves in the middle. Ehrenreich (1989) and Ortner (1991), cited by Proweller (1998), argue that the "myth of classlessness" is prominent among Americans, who tend to identify themselves as "middle-class" because they view middle-class as the "universal class with universal membership" (69). Newman (1989) claims that "the middle class is a category so broad that it encompasses everyone from white collar executives to elite unionized labor, sometimes called the labor aristocracy" (15).

Certainly, this apparent end of the working class and expansion of the middle class has affected traditional class structures. Walkerdine (2003) argues that "we no longer have a large manufacturing base which provides the pivot for an understanding of social stratification based on class divisions" (241). Lawler (2005) contends that this has, in turn, taken the respectability out of the working class and reduced them to an underclass (435). Walkerdine (2003) maintains that "the sets of political and economic changes which have led to neo-liberalism" have on the one hand freed us from "traditional ties of location, class and gender," making us completely self-produced; on the other hand, they have placed significant weight on upward mobility to the point that it has become a necessity if one wishes to maintain any respect-ability (240). In light of these changes to the economic structure and class hierarchies, the onus is on individuals from the working-class population to redefine themselves as "respectable" and not "working-class."

According to feminist theorists such as Walkerdine et al. (2001), Hey (2003) and Lawler (2005), significant to the formation of women's class-consciousness is their relation to the "feminine" and "respectability." Skeggs (1997) contends that there is considerable pressure on working-class women to appear respectable. Walkerdine (2003) elaborates on this point, arguing that working-class women are "marked more by the categorisation of their sexuality (rough/respectable/slut) and by the possibility of entry into upward mobility through their production of themselves as worthy of marriage to a middle-class man" (238). Lawler (2005) contends that respectability is defined by the feminine, stating, "Since respectability is coded as an inherent feature of 'proper' femininity, working-class women must constantly guard against being disrespectable, but no matter how carefully they do this, they are always at risk of being judged as wanting by middle-class observers" (435).

This emphasis on femininity and the feminine body is reminiscent of the discussions of girls' femininity highlighted in the previous chapter. While feminist class theory in its focus on femininity seems to hold relevance to an analysis of girl culture, two issues remain. First, feminist theorists still draw on traditional class categories, such as working class, to formulate their analyses, which brings us to the second issue: what about youth? Before we can appropriately conceptualize class in relation to girls, an examination of class in youth culture is required. The following sections examine the feminist analysis of women, femininity and class for its applicability to an analysis of girls, femininity and class.

A Classless Generation

Conceptualizing class merely in terms of paid labour is not only problematic for women, but, as McRobbie (1991) contends, "individuals are born into what are already constructed sets of social meanings which can then be worked on, developed and even transformed" (45). In other words, while youth may be assigned to particular class categories via their parents, the social meanings of these categories may become reconstituted in their peer networks. As children do not have the same access to meaningful employment as adults, they occupy or are assigned to the same class position as their parents. This hand-me-down model of class assignment has its problems. For one, it should not be assumed that children from a working-class family will have the same experiences with a particular class as their parents. After all, it is quite possible that children attach a different meaning to these social class categories, which have ultimately been defined by adults. An important question then concerns how this model of social class manifests itself in youth culture, particularly for adolescent girls.

Attempting to address this question, Eckert (1989) argues that youth have their own hierarchical system, derived from adult social class categories of lower, middle and upper class. More specifically, she contends that an important characteristic of public schools is the development of two opposing groups, "the leading crowd" versus "the rebellious crowd" (2). Eckert's research labels the leading group as the "Jocks," who are middle-class, college bound youth, and the "rebellious" group as the "Burnouts," who are predominately working-class youth. Eckert argues that, "social identity is dominated by the opposition between the two categories" (5). Interestingly, Eckert's analysis of a binary youth class structure is reminiscent of Marxian theory and its concentration on the opposition between the capitalists and the working class. While Eckert's work is significant in establishing that youth seem to have their own system of hierarchical order, she does not offer a gender analysis in her examination of Jocks and Burnouts. Therefore, it begs the question: do girls even fit into this dichotomized model of adolescence?

School Culture and Classed Identities

Proweller (1998), in her study of upper-middle-class youth culture, also asserts that youth establish their own class structures; yet, unlike Eckert, she contends that this class system varies from that of adults (66). Proweller suggests that the main site upon which youth hierarchies are produced occurs within school culture and, more specifically, the peer group (67). Certainly, this is not to say that youth are completely isolated from adult class structures. From her work on proms, Best (2000) argues that public schools contribute to the "organization of the social body, the management of social order and maintenance of class divisions" (5). Kehily (2004) asserts that an analysis of school culture is vital to our understanding of the construction of class hierarchies and more broadly, the production of gendered and sexualized identities (208). Similarly, Orenstein (1994) argues that there is a "hidden curriculum" within schools that teaches "girls to value silence and compliance" as "virtuous qualities" (35).

School culture often sets the feminine standards, in what Bettie (2003) deems the "school-sanctioned femininity that signifies middle-classness." Adopting a feminist cultural analysis, Bettie, in her research on Mexican-American girls and class identity, argues that class-consciousness is a "learned position" and, thus, "class identity comes to be known equally by markers outside of discovering one's position in paid labour" (42). Bettie (2003) also argues that girls' experiences of class are influenced by familial relations, social relations that are unrelated to employment, such as school and peer groups, as well as leisure and consumption practices dictated by popular culture (42). According to Bettie, class identity can also be contradictory in the sense that some girls may choose to present class identities that differ from their parents' socioeconomic status. Girls' class identities can be formulated through academic skills, extracurricular activities and memberships in particular peer groups; working-class girls may execute a middle-class identity and even vice versa (Bettie 2003: 50). Such a conceptualization of class suggests that girls, for instance, can have a class-consciousness that is different from adults' but meaningful in their lives.

In her work on upper-middle-class youth culture, Proweller (1998) maintains that "American adolescents are typically unfamiliar with objective measures of class and generally tend to name appearance and attitude as predictable measures of class status" (72). While it is debatable whether adults' class categories can be considered an "objective" measure of class, Proweller makes a significant point about the discrepancies between adults' and youths' conceptualizations of class. She goes on to argue that while "social class is integral to the definition of separate and distinct peer networks," these peer groups are not all "class homogeneous" (Proweller 1998: 68). In other words, the formation of youth subcultures and hierarchies encompasses a range of backgrounds, suggesting that a girl's socio-economic background does not necessarily dictate her status among her peers. Some research suggests that two additional measures of status that dictate class structures among girls are consumption and objectification, both of which relate to femininity.

The Consumption of Femininity

Since the rise of consumerism, girls and young women have been positioned as the target consumer group, where they are perceived as "excellent choice makers." Harris (2004) contends that "their confidence and success are frequently measured by their purchasing power" (166), and she argues that girls' social power, autonomy and rights are directly related to their participation in consumer consumption and the associated "skills" (166). Young women are even perceived as powerful agents in the consumer market, which has resulted in an excessive use of the slogan "girl power" by marketing companies in the advertisement of products such as fashion, technology, jewellery and even music (Harris 2004: 166). While this focus on consumer culture has created the illusion that young women have gained a sense of "citizenship status, autonomy, rights, independence and power," Harris (2004) credits McRobbie (2000) for warning that it also "disconnects feminism from politics and justice, and implies that strong and empowered girls are those who have and spend money" (167).

Bettie (2003) found an "array of gender-specific commodities [that] were used as markers of distinction among different groups of girls" (61). Hairstyles, clothes, shoes and the colours of lipstick, lip liner and nail polish emerged as key markers in a symbolic economy that is employed to express group membership and, more specifically, the feminine body that has become a resource and a site upon which difference is inscribed (62). Proweller (1998) identified similar markers, such as clothes, jewellery and automobiles, in her research with upper-middle-class girls, arguing that "conventional signifiers of femininity are reappropriated as markers of class affiliation that identify certain girls" (75).

As discussed by Hey (2003), Lawler (2005), Skeggs (1997) and Walkerdine et al. (2001), a woman's class position is largely dictated by her femininity, and according to Bettie (2003) and Proweller (1998), the same can be argued for girls. Girls may have the potential to negotiate status among their peers as long as their consumption practices reflect a particular version of femininity. A girl's ability to participate in the consumption of these gender-specific commodities referenced by Proweller (1998) and Bettie (2003) can dictate her class position. Thus, for adolescent girls, femininity and class allocation is self-produced through material consumption.

McRobbie (1991) contends that there are cultural scripts laid out by the mass media, through such products as the teen magazine, that model middle- and upper-class culture and the importance of fashion and beauty (46). Thus, a girl's status among other girls is highly contingent on her ability to consume and perform the versions of femininity as contained within these scripts.

The Feminine Body

While a girl's status is weighted heavily on consumption, what constitutes the appropriate feminine body is evaluated in accordance with patriarchal structures. Not only are girls perceived as consuming subjects, they are also objects of consumption and, more specifically, "objects of male heterosexual consumption and desire (Griffin 2004: 35). Particularly significant to these two positions of consumption are the so-called "tweenies" generation, a term derived by Brown (2001) and Ellen (2000) and defined as "prepubertal girls who are seen to constitute a novel and distinct set of targeted customers" (Griffin 2004: 35). Griffin argues that in patriarchal cultures, women's consumption is acceptable in either one of two circumstances: the first in which she is shopping for her family and the second when she is preparing herself for a man (35). This consuming female subject is particularly alarming when she is perceived as shopping for herself and acting on her own desires. Yet, Griffin concludes that "the challenge posed by girls' consumption for themselves is undermined if they can be represented preparing their (girl) selves for a (male) other; the actual or potential 'boyfriend'"(35).

Thus, shopping is perceived as a means of expressing one's femininity (status) and becoming the "object of the male gaze." Yet, Ellen (2000) makes the argument that the media panic over "tweenies" lies in their representation as prepubertal and therefore, too young to be seeking out boyfriends. Consequently, they become viewed as insatiable consumers, who are "inappropriately (hetero) sexualized for their age" and as Griffin (2004) contends, "this is one of several unsettling aspects of the young consuming female subject" (35).

Even as young girls are being perceived as powerful agents in the consumer market, this power is undermined by patriarchal structures. In other words, the pursuit of male approval and validation of the feminine body becomes the driving force behind girls' participation in the consumer culture. Thus, girls may negotiate their status relative to other girls through the evaluation of femininities; yet, their greatest means of power lies in an ability to capture and retain male attention through feminine performances that play on sexual appeal. However, not all girls conform to the same model of femininity, as Chesney-Lind and Brown (1999), Laidler and Hunt (2001) and Jiwani (2006) maintain. In other words, different versions of femininity are an expression of a girl's gendered, racialized and classed identities.

Discourses of Difference

Jiwani (2006) asserts that in analyses of violence it is often the case that one structure of domination is privileged over another, and she cites patriarchy and race as examples (202). She also argues that hierarchical structures of power are reinforced through "the subordination of one group — its inferiorization and the naturalization of that inferiorization" (203). This naturalization of inferiorization is illustrated in Proweller's (1998) discussion of "whiteness" as the raceless subjectivity (98). Proweller draws on a quote from Richard Dyer (1988) to clarify her point: "The colourless multi-colouredness of whiteness secures white power by making it hard, especially for white people and their media, to 'see' whiteness. This, of course, also makes it hard to analyse" (46). Similarly, Ali (2003) contends that "the analysis of working-class girls' subjectivities" is often "set within a 'white' framework" (273).

These structures of dominance are further exemplified in Batacharya's (2004) work on the trial of Kelly Ellard for the murder of Reena Virk. Batacharya argues that the defence counsel relied on the privileging of white, middle-class femininity to present Ellard as a "good, middle-class girl who had merely fallen into a bad peer group" (75). According to Batacharya (2004), Ellard's "violence is unimaginable not because of the brutality of her crime, but because of her social location as a white, middle-class girl" (76). Thus, not only are there structures of dominance that reinforce men's superiority over women, but there are also structures of dominance that are manifested within the boundaries of femininity — in this case, through the constituents of racial hierarchies. Batacharya (2004) refers to this particular structure of dominance as "hegemonic femininity" (63).

In conjunction with these arguments, Bettie (2003) argues that girls are "living in a society stratified by race/ethnicity, class, and sexuality as much as gender." The girls involved in Bettie's study "performed different versions of femininity that were integrally linked to and inseparable from their class and racial/ethnic performances" (5). She argues that "the body has long been the only raw material or capital with which impoverished and working-class women have to work," which inevitably, "secures their subordinate place in class hierarchy" (93). Evidently, the feminine body is central to girls' class-consciousness, where stricter boundaries are usually placed on working-class girls. Thus, for Bettie, girls' performances of femininity are dependent on their social and economic circumstances and their "class-specific perform-ances of femininity" (97). Proweller (1998), referencing the work of Rosaldo (1993), claims that social borders such as class, race and gender are sites of "creative cultural production that capture the fluid and dynamic quality of identity formation" (66). Thus, structures of gender, class and race shape girls' diverse and ever-changing performances of femininity.

Lending support to the claim that race and class structures are equally important to an analysis of femininity, Griffin (2004) draws on an example of a pre-teen magazine in Britain, entitled *Mad about Boys*, to illustrate how whiteness resonates as a dominant force in the dictation of femininity in popular culture (36). The magazine, for example, provides a section on the practice of straightening "wild hair." Griffin (2004) interprets this as straightening the "nappy" hair in girls of colour so they will "conform to dominant constructions of 'attractive' and desirable hair as smooth and glossy" (Griffin 2004: 38). This suggests that what constitutes feminine standards is highly racialized.

In line with Griffin's work, Bettie (2003) argues that girls' performances of femininity are highly influenced by race and ethnicity (55). Crothers, Field and Kolbert (2005) also attest to the importance of girls' racial and ethnic backgrounds in the construction of feminine identities (349). Griffin (2004) references Reay's (2001) work in making the argument that "girlhood is constituted through multiple and frequently competing discourses, which position girls and young women in different ways, and are shaped by class and 'race' as well as gender and sexuality" (32). Similarly, Proweller (1998) discusses the notion of "the borderland," which she defines as "a site where differences growing up at the intersection of salient borders and border zones of class, race, ethnicity, gender, and sexuality, are continuously negotiated and worked through" (66).

While Bettie (2003) contends that feminine performances are highly influenced by structures of class and race she also maintains that race is often displaced. For instance, "the tendency to see working-class girls as shaped most by gender may occur precisely because of the particular working-class racialized version of femininity they are performing" (Bettie 2003: 92).

This displacement of race among the girls exemplifies the meaning behind Jiwani's term, "erasing race," where structures of race are overshadowed by structures of gender or, in this case, class. Bettie (2003) discusses girls' use of phrases such as "acting white" as a term that does not encompass all whites but rather refers specifically to a middle-class version of whiteness (83). Thus, while particular performances are racialized, they also imply a particular class performance and these class performances are racially coded. For instance, Bettie found that the girls' middle- or working-class performances were interpreted differently depending on the race/ethnicity of the "performer and the "reader." She concludes that this is due to the "race-specific meanings" that are associated with particular ideas about "authentic" racial and ethnic identities and hierarchies (85). Hence, the phrase "acting white" does imply a class performance, even though the girls may understand it in terms of a racial identity. Bettie asserts that race and class are "mutually implicated" and "read in relationship to one another," which can obscure our understanding of both these structures (86).

While it is important to recognize that girls' experiences of class will vary based on their racial and ethnic backgrounds, Ali (2003) cautions that in analyzing race and ethnicity in line with social class, we must not rely on racial stereotypes to predict classed experiences. In other words, we should not assume that there is one "Black" experience of middle-classness versus one "white" experience of middle-classness. Ali argues that it is problematic to assume that particular versions of femininity are inherently characteristic of certain racial or ethnic backgrounds (280).

Indeed, race and ethnicity are important concepts to consider in the analysis of class identity. However, in her analysis of "the interplay of ethnicity, race and class in the production of femininities," Ali discusses the difficulty in analyzing these three "aspects of identity" (269). She argues that because of the complexities of these concepts, "there is no neat theoretical frameworks for such positions" (270). Similarly, Jiwani (2006) contends that there is no "additive approach" to analyzing structures of race, class and gender and "the confluence of these structures of domination results in differential outcomes and in constitution of difference that does not resemble an outcome that is simply additive" (203).

Jiwani (2006) also maintains that there is no "essentialist framework" for understanding or analyzing difference. The important point to be made here is that structures of dominance impact girls differently — both in terms of the structures of dominance that define girls' existence and the discourses of denial that manifest hierarchies of power.

While my initial research questions involved a focus on class and girl aggression, given the complex connection between race and class, it is not possible to analyze class without acknowledging multiple structures of dominance present in girls' lives. For this reason, in this study, the class analysis also focuses on structures of gender and race in relation to girls' aggression.

Research Implications and Questions

Given that mainstream femininity, a primary measure of girls' popularity, is a product of white, middle-class culture, white girls from middle-class backgrounds seem to have the upper hand when negotiating their status among other girls. This is not to say that minority girls and/or girls from lower-class backgrounds cannot achieve popularity but that girls' popularity is highly influenced by structures of race and class. Girls' "hidden" aggression does not directly challenge structures of patriarchy and the privileging of male aggression; therefore, it offers some girls the opportunity to gain a sense of social power while also conforming to traditional notions of femininity. It would seem that meanness is more common among popular girls of white, middle-class status than unpopular girls of minority and/or lower-class status. In line with this, it would appear that girls from lower-class backgrounds and/or minority-status are more likely to use overt aggression, but these girls must also learn to carefully negotiate their feminine performances in line with their aggression should they wish to avoid social rejection.

There are important research questions that arise from the literature surrounding popularity, power, class, race and femininity. The work of Merton (1997), Lease, Kennedy and Axelrod (2002), Rose, Swenson and Walker (2004), Cillessen and Mayeux (2004) and Phillips (2003) on girl aggression led to me to investigate the following questions concerning the relationship between meanness and popularity:

- Are hidden forms of aggression such as gossip, peer alienation and dirty looks more common among popular, higher-status girls?
- How does a girl's status affect whether she expresses or constrains her aggression?
- Does a girl's status affect her use of violence and/or overt aggression as a defence mechanism?
- Do girls benefit from using hidden forms of aggression? Overt aggression?

Campbell (1993), Gilligan (1993), Artz (1998), Brown (2003) and Crothers, Field and Kolbert (2005) analyze gender inequality and patriarchy in relation to girls' meanness and the suppression of their aggression, and this work prompted questions related to girls' power:

- How do feelings of powerlessness affect how girls express their aggression?
- What does power represent to girls? Do girls associate power with physical force?

Miller and White (2004), Batacharya (2004), Chesney-Lind and Pasko (2004) and Jiwani (2006) argue that gender alone does not sufficiently account for the different forms of aggression exhibited by girls. Rather, an analysis of girls' aggression and violence requires an examination of multiple power relations as manifested through structures of race and class as well as gender. This leads to the following questions:

- How do structures of race and class shape girls' perceptions of aggression?

- Do these structures influence how girls express their aggression?
- How do perceptions of girls' aggression vary along race and class divisions?
- How do girls' lessons in aggression compare along race and class divisions?

Some works suggested that femininity is the main site upon which a girl's status is determined. Proweller (1998), Bettie (2003), Griffin (2004), Batacharya (2004), Crothers, Field and Kolbert (2005) and Jiwani (2006) claim that there are hierarchies of femininity dictated by race, class and gender relations. In line with this, Best (2000), Currie and Kelly (2006) and Jiwani (2006) identify important connections between femininity and girls' power negotiations. Simmons (2002), Brown (2003), Miller and White (2004) and Currie and Kelly (2006) argue that girls' aggression is constrained by feminine standards. However, Chesney-Lind and Brown (1999), Laidler and Hunt (2001) and Jiwani (2006) claim that what constitutes femininity is influenced by structures of class, race and gender; thus, girls negotiate their femininity accordingly. This discourse surrounding femininity led me to ask:

- How important are feminine standards of "niceness" in determining how a girl will aggress?
- Is a girl's participation in aggression reflective of her feminine ideals?
- Does femininity dictate a girl's status?
- Do girls negotiate their aggression in line with their femininity?

Conclusion

While some of these research questions have been addressed in previous research, most of these studies have involved white girls from middle-class backgrounds who are typically between the ages of fifteen and seventeen. This is clearly problematic as it suggests that our understanding of girls' aggression is reflective of only one demographic of girls, thereby ignoring important differences shaped by structures of race, class and age. Indeed, there is every reason to believe that there are theoretically important differences between young girls' views of aggression and those of older, teenage girls. In discussions with girls aged fifteen to seventeen for my honours research, age appeared to have important implications for girls' perspectives of mean or aggressive behaviour. These older girls had already begun their transition into womanhood, and they seemed to be leaving aspects of girl culture behind and emulating adult ways of thinking and acting. Certainly, this speaks to the need for research that draws on the experiences and perspectives of girls who have yet to enter the teen years and are fully immersed in girl culture.

Note

1. Social class is a "sociological concept with a variety of definitions depending on which theoretical perspective is used. It generally refers to one's economic position or standing in a particular social structure or society." Another term similar to social class is socioeconomic status, which refers to "a person's social standing or position in terms of their education, occupation and income" (Bell 2002: 282).

Chapter Three

Methodologies for Girl Talk

Rooted in feminist qualitative research methodology, this chapter outlines the focus group methodology I employed in obtaining a girl perspective on issues concerning girls' meanness and aggression. Following an introduction of the girl participants, the chapter provides a detailed discussion of the focus group sessions and the second method of data collection, the reflection journals. The concluding section of this chapter offers a comprehensive discussion of the methodological issues that arose during the research.

A Girl Perspective

A pioneer in the field of girl studies, Gilligan (1990) makes a strong case for the importance of a girl perspective in research in that she praises the value of girls' knowledge for its ability to explain circumstances and phenomena unique to girl culture. She asserts that it is a type of knowledge that is "gleaned by seeing and listening, by piecing together thoughts and feelings, sounds and glances, responses and reactions until they compose a pattern, compelling in its explanatory power and often intricate in its psychological logic" (14). Yet, Brown (2003) contends that girls' voices can offer more than just a psychological understanding of individual circumstances; they can also educate us about the social world in which we live. According to Chesney-Lind and Sheldon (1998), "An appreciation of a young woman's experience of girlhood, particularly one that attends to the special problems of girls at the margin, is long overdue" (6).

Gilligan and Brown (1992) argue that by studying girls, "we could arrive at a better understanding of women's psychology" (9). While researching the stages of female development is certainly a valuable endeavour, there is more to be said for the importance of girl-centred research than simply what we can learn about women. After all, girls have their own sets of experiences and perspectives. Not only is it important to study girls in their own right, but girls should be empowered to speak for themselves on issues that directly affect their lives. Indeed, Brown (2003) expresses this by saying, "conversations with girls, especially when they feel safe enough to speak openly, offer more chance for girls' private and public struggles to be expressed and understood" (6).

From feminist methodology emerged the "standpoint" approach, which credits Dorothy Smith as its most infamous developer. Smith (1987) contends that the standpoint approach is a method that "at the outset of inquiry, creates the space for an absent subject, and an absent experience that is to be filled with the presence and spoken experience of actual [girls] speaking of and in the actualities of their everyday worlds" (107). The feminist standpoint approach is reproduced in a "girl perspective" methodology that recognizes the importance of girls' narratives in the face of increasing feminist research involving women. Certainly, feminist qualitative methodology aims to give a voice to girls' "gendered experiences" of violence and aggression (Chesney-Lind and Pasko (eds.) 2004: 45).

Brown's (2003) work on "girlfighting" employs a "girl perspective" methodology in that she talked to girls about issues such as competition, anger and aggression, friendships and femininity. In defence of a research method that gives girls a voice in matters that affect them, Brown argues that "girls have an intense desire to be recognized, to be heard" (86). Burman (2004) suggests that "talking with girls" is a research strategy that "entails listening to girls... as authorities about their own experiences and representing their voices in text" (83). Barron (2000) makes a similar argument about talking to youth: "More than asking their opinion, we must respect their responses... it is time for us to appreciate young people as 'knowers' of their situation" (123). Chesney-Lind and Sheldon (1998) argue: "The early years of life set the stage for girls to experience gender as identity, as role, as rule, and ultimately, as an institutional web of expectations that defines women, especially young women, as subordinate to men" (6). In talking to girls, we can begin to understand the ways in which patriarchy manifests itself in their lives. Reflected in issues such as eating disorders, self-mutilation, sexual violence, drug addiction, alcoholism and teen pregnancy, girls experience the tyranny of patriarchal society from birth, through childhood and adolescence, and into womanhood. Undoubtedly, the only way that we can begin to address the multitude of issues facing girls would be to stop speculating and let girls do the talking.

A common feature of girl culture is that girls do things together in friendship groups (Brown 2003: 52). Therefore, I chose as my primary research tool, focus groups rather than individual interviews, because this would mimic a conversation among a group of friends. Litosseliti (2003) argues that focus groups are "useful for revealing through interaction the beliefs, attitudes, experiences and feelings of participants" (16) and "focus group methodology allows for flexibility in examining a range of topics with a variety of individuals" (17). Focus groups offered the flexibility to open the discussions to broader issues surrounding girl status, power and femininity. This method also provided the structure to centre in on the most critical issues concerning girl aggression and class by posing specific questions.

Recognizing that the group dynamic could affect some girls' ability to speak openly, it was important to provide an alternative outlet where the girls had free-range to share their thoughts and opinions. This was the rationalization for introducing an additional research method, the reflection journals. The girls were asked to keep reflection journals over the duration of the research period, and they were given questions concerning the focus group topics to discuss in these journals. As well, I invited the girls to share stories, experiences and additional thoughts about particular issues in these journals or to offer feedback on the focus groups.

The Girls

The twenty-four girls, aged eight to eleven, were all members of a non-profit youth organization that runs after-school programs in local communities. The research took place at two locations of this organization, both of which are situated in areas outside a larger metropolitan area and serve mainly lower-income families.[11] According to the staff at these locations, the girls came from predominantly working-class families. The majority of the girls I interviewed were white, and approximately one-quarter of the girls were Black or mixed-race, with both a Black and white biological parent. Upon first meeting the girls, I gathered that appearance was of primary importance to them as it seemed to be an indicator of popularity. In other words, the girls with slim bodies and well-groomed hairstyles, who sported the latest fashions in name-brand clothing, seemed to occupy the popular positions among their peers. I refer to these girls as the "higher-status" girls. In contrast, the "lower-status" girls were those who did not possess culturally "desirable" feminine traits such as smooth, straight hair, a clear complexion, a slim body or material commodities such as name-brand clothing. While the girls may have come from similar class backgrounds, their status among one another varied considerably.

The focus groups were conducted in rooms at the organizations where the girls were accustomed to meeting for a variety of after-school activities. Most of the girls remained for the duration of the study, although several of the girls did not attend every session. The staff, as well as the girls themselves, always assured me that these absences were due to commitments such as Girl Guides, music lessons, school plays, ballet or cheerleading practice. The girls who participated in these extracurricular activities would often demonstrate their talents in the focus group settings by performing cheers, dancing, singing, reciting lines from a play or playing a musical instrument. On several occasions, the girls offered to make up plays and perform them for me. Throughout the duration of the study, the girls became quite animated about topics such as clothing, shopping, boys and celebrity idols such as Paris Hilton and the female music group, The Pussycat Dolls. Overall, the girls appeared quite comfortable with the focus group discussions and completely genuine in expressing their thoughts. I never had the impression that they were trying to please me by saying things that they thought I wanted to hear.

The Focus Groups

Before making contact with the girls, the staff at this organization handed out parental consent forms to any of the girls that were interested in participating. At the same time, the girls were given participant consent forms. The organization expressed an interest in speaking to the girls themselves about my research and the consent forms, prior to me meeting the girls. Thus, I met with the staff at both research locations to discuss the details of my research as well as explain the purpose of the consent forms. The staff was asked to emphasize to the girls that their participation in the study was voluntary and should they decide to participate they would have to return both consent forms signed to the organization prior to the commencement of the research. I arranged for a staff person at both locations to be available to talk to any of the girls should any problems arise during the focus group sessions. Upon our first meeting, the girls were reassured that they were there voluntarily and that they were free to choose the discussions in which they wished to participate. Following this, I spoke to all the girls about the importance of confidentiality and anonymity. In doing so, we came to a mutual understanding that in signing their participant consent forms, they were agreeing to respect the privacy of the other girls and keep what was said in the sessions to themselves. As well, I also explained to them that with me signing these forms, I was also promising to keep each girl's identity secret. To ensure the anonymity of the girls, I have used pseudonyms for their names and any other names referred in their stories.

Four sets of focus groups were conducted at the two different locations with four sets of girls over the duration of six weeks. All the focus groups were recorded and ranged in duration from thirty minutes to upwards of two hours. Rather than merely presenting the girls with a series of questions, they were shown movie clips and pictorial images to create a more relaxed setting aimed at stimulating more natural dialogue between the girls. The clips and images reflected the kinds of images that have been problematized in the mainstream as girls' meanness. Utilizing visuals offered the potential for focused discussions about specific issues and concepts surrounding aspects of girl culture that were being portrayed in the clips and images. Each group of girls participated in four different focus group sessions, which corresponded to the four themes developed in the last chapter: "Meanness and Popularity," "Girl Power?" "Race and Class" and finally, "Femininity." Once the girls' viewed the clips, I posed a series of prompt questions to spark group discussions about the visual clips and images.

Focus Group 1: Meanness and Popularity

In the first focus group sessions, the girls were presented with clips from the movie *Odd Girl Out*, a film that addresses the issue of girl bullying by depicting a teenage girl's descent from popularity when her best friend decides to isolate her from their group. The focus group discussion centred on clips from this movie that featured incidents of seemingly popular girls being mean to another girl. The girls were asked the following questions:

Clip #1: A group of popular girls, Vanessa, Stacey and Nicki, make a negative comment about another girl's skirt as they pass her in the hallway.

> What do you think of these girls?
> Do you think their behaviour is aggressive? Mean?
> Do you think they are popular? Why? Why not?
> Do you think one girl in this group stands out as the leader more than the other two? Why? Why not?
> What makes a girl popular?
> What kinds of things are important to popular girls?
> What makes a girl unpopular?
> What do popular girls do when they are angry? What about unpopular girls?
> Are there "rules" around how you can behave as a girl? If so, where do girls learn these rules?

Clip #2: Vanessa, Stacey and Nicki tease another girl found sitting at "their" table in the cafeteria.

> Why do you think these girls do not like the girl sitting at their table?

Clip #3: Nicki and Stacey watch Vanessa talking to a boy and then when Stacey yells out to them to wait up, they do not acknowledge her.

> What was that about?
> Do you think Nicki and Stacey heard Vanessa calling out to them? If so, why did they keep walking?

Clip #4: Vanessa attempts to sit down with her friends at their table; however the girls tell her that there is no room for her.

> Why is Vanessa not allowed to sit with her friends?
> What do you think of her friends' behaviour?
> Do you think they have the right to be angry with her?

Clip #5: While playing soccer in gym class, Nicki confronts Vanessa, calling her a "slut" and a "whore."

> Why do you think Nicki called Vanessa a slut and a whore?

Do you think she is those things?
Do you think Nicki's behaviour was aggressive?

Clip #6: A group of girls show Vanessa a computer-animated image of herself eating muffins and growing larger with every bite.

Why do you think the girls are picking on Vanessa's weight?
Do girls have coded messages? If so, what are they?

Clip #7: Vanessa confesses to her mom that she is having difficulty at school with her friends. Vanessa's mom suggests she talk to Stacey but Vanessa rejects that idea, claiming it will only make things worse.

Why do you think Vanessa will not confront Stacey?
Would that make the situation worse or better?
Do you think most girls hide their anger?

Clip #8: Vanessa confronts Stacey at school and Stacey acts friendly and nonchalant with her.

Why do you think Stacey was nice to Vanessa?
Do you think girls smile and act nice even when something is bothering them? If so, why do they do this? Why wouldn't a girl just go up and punch someone if they were bothering her?

Clip #9: Vanessa enters the cafeteria. Stacey smiles as Vanessa approaches the table. The other girls sitting at the table refuse to let Vanessa sit with them. Vanessa slams down her cafeteria tray on the table and runs off to the washroom where all the girls follow her and insult her as she sits in one of the stalls.

Is there any behaviour in that clip that you think is aggressive? Why or Why not?
Why do you think those girls acted like that towards Vanessa? What is it about?
Do you think Stacey was just pretending to be Vanessa's friend again? If yes, why would she do that?
Are there any benefits in pretending to be another girl's friend?

Focus Group 2: Girl Power?

The second focus group session with the girls was centred on the concept of power, and I opened the discussion up with the questions: What is power? How do girls show their power? How do boys and men show their power? These questions were aimed at determining whether girls perceive differences in power dynamics in relation to gender. Following this, I showed the girls a picture of three popular girls — one Black and two white, standing together in what appears to be a school hallway. Interestingly, this image was retrieved from the Google Image Search Engine by typing in "popular girls." After viewing this picture, I asked the girls a series of questions:

What do you think of these girls?
Would you say they are popular? Why or why not?
Do you think these girls have power? Why or why not?
What makes a girl powerful?
What makes a girl powerless?

Following this, the girls were shown an actual news photo of two Black girls fighting and asked:

Do you think these girls are popular? Why or why not?
What do you think this fight is about?
Why do you think some girls fight and others don't?
Does fighting make girls powerful?

To stimulate further discussion about power, I showed the girls a clip from the movie *Mean Girls*. In contrast to *Odd Girl Out*, this movie tackles the issue of "girl bullying" in a more satirical manner. The clips featured incidents involving a group of girls referred to by their peers as the "Plastics," for their presumably perfect, Barbie-doll-like appearances, and addressed issues surrounding popularity and standards of femininity. After viewing the clips, I asked the following questions:

What makes the Plastics popular?
Do you think they have power? Why or Why not?
Do you think most schools have groups of girls like the Plastics?
Do most girls have rules among their friends? If so, what kind of rules?
Are there rules around boys?
Are there rules around being good?
How important is it for a girl to be pretty?
Do pretty girls have power?
What happens when a girl is not pretty?

Following this, the girls were shown two brief clips from the Canadian documentary *It's a Girls' World*, which also addresses the issue of "social bullying" among girls. These two clips feature girls talking about power in which one girl comments that girls "always take the side of a powerful girl" and another girl conveys that putting another girl down offers a sense of power. I then asked these questions:

Do you think acting mean makes girls feel powerful?
What other ways do girls feel power?
What is a powerful girl? Who is she?

Focus Group 3: Race and Class
The third focus group session addressed issues of race and class. To introduce this topic, I showed the girls a clip from the movie *Save the Last Dance*, which features a physical fight between a white girl and a Black girl during

a basketball game in gym class. After viewing this clip, I asked the girls:

Do you think these girls are aggressive?
Is one girl more aggressive than the other?
What is going on in that situation?
Why do you think that fight started?
Do you think those girls are popular? Why or why not?
Is it common for popular girls to have physical fights like that?
Wouldn't they be afraid to get into trouble by adults?

This clip also opened the discussion to issues surrounding girls' anger and the girls were asked the following:

How do girls show anger differently?
What kinds of things affect how girls deal with their anger? Money? Family? Friends? Grades in school?

I also asked girls about girls' lessons in aggression:

Where do girls learn how to fight?
What are girls taught about aggression and anger?
Do you think there are any situations where fighting is necessary for girls?
Do you think it was okay for those girls to behave like they did? Why or why not?
What kinds of girls do you think fight the most?

I referred the girls to the clips they had viewed from *Odd Girl Out, Mean Girls* and *It's a Girls' World* and asked if they felt that anyone was not being represented in these films. This served the purpose of establishing that all the "mean girl" characters in these films were white girls. I asked the girls:

Do you think meanness is an issue with white girls?
Do you think that girls of different races behave differently?
Does the colour of a girl's skin affect what she is taught about aggression and how others treat her?[22]

Focus Group 4: Femininity

The final focus group session addressed structures of femininity. The girls were shown two opposing images: one was an apparent "good girl," featuring a girl with blonde hair, pigtails, fashionable clothing and a friendly smile. The other image depicted a stereotypical "bad girl," who possessed blue spiky hair, facial piercings, dark eye make-up, mismatched clothing and a scowl on her face. As with the "popular girls" image, both of these images were retrieved from Google Image Engine Search by typing in "good girl" and then "bad girl." As I showed the girls each image, I posed the following questions:

How would you describe this girl?
Do you think she is likeable? Why? Why not?
What kinds of things are important to her?

Do you think she has lots of friends?
Do you think she has a boyfriend?
Do you think she is aggressive? Mean?

Using these images as a stimulus to further the discussion surrounding femininities, I also asked the following questions:

What do you think these girls have in common?
What makes them different?
What would you consider to be a good girl?
Do you think girls care about being good girls? Why or why not?
Is it important to be a nice girl? Why or why not?
Do you think girls care about what other girls think? Why or why not?
What kind of girl does not care about being a good girl?
What would you consider a bad girl?
What kinds of things are girlie? What do you like about girlieness?
What don't you like about girlieness?
What makes a girl not girlie?
Are girls who fight less girlie? Why or why not?
What do you like best about being a girl? What do you like the least?

The Reflection Journals

In the initial reflection journal entry, each girl was asked to create a profile of herself by talking about her likes, dislikes, extracurricular activities, hobbies, favourite subject(s) in school and, most importantly, family unit (including parents, siblings, pets). Following this, at the end of each focus group, I asked the girls reflection journal questions, which they wrote down and could later respond to in their journals. At the final focus group, I gave the girls a piece of paper listing all the reflection journal questions. These questions addressed the main issues in the focus group sessions:

Why do girls act mean?
What do girls do when they get angry?
Do girls hide their anger?
How do you think boys and girls act differently?
What makes a girl powerful?
What makes a girl popular?
How does skin colour affect a girl's life?
How does being poor affect a girl's life?
Why do girls fight?
Is it important for a girl to be nice?
What is the hardest part about being a girl?
Are girls who fight less girlie?

I instructed the girls that responding to the reflection journal questions was voluntarily. As well, I told them that they were welcome to share additional thoughts or personal narratives concerning any of the topics that were discussed in the focus groups, if they so desired. I collected the reflection journals from the girls two weeks after the final focus group session was finished in order to give the girls time to make their last entry.

Methodological Issues

With any research there are methodological issues that need to be addressed. These issues arose both before and during the research process and centred on ethical concerns, the researcher and participant relationship, and the specific research methods that were employed.

Ethical Concerns

Although ethics is always a significant consideration in any research where human subjects are involved, ethical concerns are considerably heightened with child participants. First and foremost, the topic for my research, girl aggression, was subject to some controversy with the ethics committee, which was concerned about a potential for "emotional responses" from the participants, due to the topic's "serious nature." The committee presented a number of "what if" scenarios, such as, "Do you think there is any possibility that participation in the focus groups might itself become a cause of bullying?" The mere structure of this question insinuates that one should not conduct research on girl bullying and aggression because participation in such a study could potentially increase this behaviour.

As anticipated, there were "emotional" issues that arose throughout the research period. The girls consistently talked about injustices they suffered in their everyday lives. More specifically, they expressed feelings of frustration about not being heard or respected by one another, by boys and by adults. In turn, the girls shared strong feelings of inadequacy and powerlessness that they felt were hopeless to remedy. Emotions overflowed during the last focus group session with the girls. Within a half hour of the session starting, one girl left the room crying. While I was consoling her, she shared with me that she was feeling excluded, saying, "no one ever listens to me." After talking with this girl and assigning her to be my "special helper" for the evening, we made our way back into the room with the other girls. Some time later, another girl was out in the hallway crying; she too was feeling excluded by some of the girls. After consoling three different girls about these same feelings, I got us all back together as a group.

Each girl was given the opportunity to talk, and all ten of the girls at the final session shared feelings of exclusion, powerlessness and inadequacy. All the girls' emotions were reflective of that first girl who left the room crying, "no one ever listens to me," including parents, teachers and peers. Here I was, a researcher, amidst all of this emotion and listening to their words, and specifically, "no one ever listens to us, except you." It nearly brought tears to my eyes, and I realized that this is what feminist qualitative research is all about. If I had succeeded at nothing else in this research, at least I had provided an avenue for the girls' silenced voices to be heard.

In a roundabout way, my research did spark emotional responses among my participants; however, this was not necessarily a negative thing as these emotional responses seemed to be beneficial to the participants. The girls participating in the research had an opportunity to share their thoughts, frustrations and stories as well as learn that there are individuals who do value what girls have to say.

The Researcher-Participant Relationship

Another important obstacle to be addressed is the researcher-participant relationship. Certainly, the responses given by the girls may have been answers that they felt would be favourable to me rather than what they really thought. Gilligan and Brown (1992) discuss the barrier they encountered between the researchers and the girls they studied as one of collaboration and rehearsed answers:

> The girls responded to our research by aligning themselves against the intrusion. In private, we later discovered, they shared their memories of the questions with one another and their parents, reassured their soon-to-be interviewed friends, began to prepare for their interviews as best they could by taking in bits of information gathered here and there and rehearsing their "lines." And we could not miss the irony. We came to the school to learn from girls; our work depended on girls' willingness to speak to us from their experiences. (9)

In recognition of this problem, I made attempts to create an informal setting. Questions and discussions were in a language to which the girls could relate, I dressed casually so as not to appear as an authority figure and snacks were supplied at the group discussions. I also requested a secluded location within the building that would be conducive to open discussions with the girls.

I was also faced with a more personal struggle, commonplace in feminist fieldwork: the close bond that is often formed between the participant and the researcher. Indeed, moral and ethical dilemmas are inherent in feminist research. Devault (1996) argues that while feminists are often attracted to research methods that offer the possibilities for direct and personal interactions with participants, they must also grapple with methodological and ethical concerns that would not necessarily present themselves in quantitative research methods, such as with surveys or questionnaires. Indeed, I struggled myself with moral questions, such as, "how do I effectively walk away from these girls after building a close, trusting relationship with them?" Especially in light of the fact that the girls had come to look up to me as an adult figure who listened to them. Because of this, I felt a particularly strong sense of responsibility and obligation to the girls.

To complicate matters further, one of the girls' mothers approached me about mentoring her daughter, as the mother felt her daughter was in need of "a positive young woman role model in her life." Although the mother's request to "mentor" her daughter was flattering and even tempting, I declined her proposal, explaining that it would be a conflict of interest due to our researcher-participant relationship. It also occurred to me that this would be an informal arrangement between the mother and myself, and, thus, there would be no institution to safeguard me against issues that could potentially arise. I decided that the best way to further these interactions would be through the institution and through email correspondence. All the girls were given my email address should they wish to write to me. Several of the girls do write on occasion. In addition, the directors at both research locations were receptive to my request to continue visiting the girls at their convenience. However, after visiting both locations twice since my research ended, it seemed that only the girls at one location enjoyed my visits. A possible reason for this may be that the girls at the other location have a program specifically designed for girls that is headed by a young woman, whereas the girls at the other organization have no such program or any sort of female role model to which they can turn.

Devault (1996) claims that "some writers... have suggested that feminist fieldwork should include special efforts to give something back to participants, or strategies for working with local groups to make change" (38). To this end, I accepted an invitation to present a workshop at a national conference headed by the organization in which I did my research. Using my findings as the foundation from which to develop the workshop, I provided administrators, front-line workers and volunteers of this particular organization with concepts that could be applied to the development of interactive strategies for working with girls on a day-to-day basis.

Talking versus Writing

While the girls seemed initially receptive to the reflection journal idea, only a small proportion of the girls returned their journals at the end. This suggests two things. First, journals may be better suited to older girls, as it seemed that many of the girls were just developing their writing skills. Second, diary writing may be more common among lower status girls; the girls who returned their journals were girls who seemed "less popular" among their peers. These were the same girls who indicated that they rarely have an opportunity to speak for themselves. Thus, they may have grown accustomed to writing in a diary as an outlet for expressing their thoughts, feelings and frustrations. Certainly, while writing can be a therapeutic activity in girl world, it does not compare to the liberating experience that was obtained through the girl talk in the focus groups.

I had naively assumed that many of the answers to my research questions would be addressed in the girls' journal entries because the anonymity of their written thoughts would evoke fewer inhibitions than the focus group setting. In fact, the girls appeared more than willing to share openly in the focus group discussions. They spent much of the time competing for the floor to tell a story, make a comment or respond to a question. As well, they did not hesitate in challenging another girl's statement if they did not agree with what she had said. Undoubtedly, this speaks to the strong desire that young girls have to share their thoughts, stories and opinions as well as the need for more research that empowers girls to talk and be heard.

Conclusion

Offering a girl perspective, especially one that focuses on younger girls, is rare in research. Through the focus group discussions with the girls and their reflection journal entries, my research provides a candid glimpse into girl world. While some methodological issues arose during this process, sometimes even providing a new perspective on these issues (such as the problem of emotion), the integrity of a feminist qualitative research methodology was upheld. My time spent with the girls exposed narratives of frustration, oppression and powerlessness as well as resiliency that have important implications for our knowledge of girl aggression.

Notes

1. For the purpose of protecting the girls' anonymity, I have chosen to omit the name of the organization and the exact location of the research.
2. While I have defined "race" as a socially constructed concept, the wording of these questions may appear to contradict this. However, recognizing that these girls were as young as eight, it was important to keep the questions straightforward and simplistic. As well, the purpose of this question was to uncover the girls' perceptions of "race" and girls' aggression.

Chapter Four

Popularity and Power

In this chapter, I explore important discrepancies between the girls' views and adults' conceptualizations of meanness. I examine girls' rationale for mean behaviour and its prevalence in their lives. In addition, I explore the role of meanness in girls' negotiations of status and power in a patriarchal society. The latter part of the chapter outlines the girls' narratives of injustices and investigates how hierarchies of power play out in girl culture.

Meanness Is Not Aggression

Although the girls' overall reaction to the girls' mean behaviour in the film *Odd Girl Out* could be summed up in comments such as "That's rude!" and "Yeah, that was sooooo mean!" they were not convinced that behaviour such as gossip, name-calling and meanness should be considered aggressive. One girl argued, "They were not into punching and hitting." When asked, "What is aggression?" the girls gave responses such as "It means anger with actions," "Angry people!" "I think it means people that just wanna hurt them," and they used examples such as "pushing and hitting." When asked whether mean behaviour is aggressive, most of the girls responded with a "no." One girl argued, "Well it's not really aggressive because she didn't push her but it's kinda rude and aggressive... maybe." In sharing a personal narrative about bullying, one girl commented, "I don't get like really bullied at my school, but I do get called names and stuff," suggesting that she did not consider "name-calling" bullying.

This is not to say that the girls were not aware of the adult discourse surrounding relational aggression and girl bullying. As one girl argued, "I think girls have more like... emotional bullying and like... boys do like fighting and stuff and girls insult with names." Another girl said, "I know the two kinds of bullying, physical and verbal." One girl even commented, "Girls at our age are very emotional." Certainly, the girls recognize that these are adults' perceptions of this behaviour. Several of the girls even admitted to being labelled by teachers and parents as bullies because they were known to gossip and, in the words of one adult that I spoke with at the organization, "She treats other girls very badly." In recalling an incident at school, where a group of friends were teasing a girl about her appearance, one of these so-called "girl bullies" stated, "Well the principal called it bullying, but I don't know." In discussing adults' reactions to so-called "girl bullying," the girls remarked that, "They think it's, what do you call it?... verbal abuse," "they just call it bullying but they don't know..." "They don't know how hard it is" and "they never see from our point of view, they see from their own." Indeed, there was a general consensus among the girls that adults are quick to label behaviour and make judgment calls without putting it in the context of girls' everyday lives. This suggests that girls' conceptualization of meanness is much different from that of adults, a difference that undoubtedly has repercussions in terms of how meanness is addressed by adults. Ultimately, adults have problematized this behaviour without understanding its meaning in girl culture. The girls' comments also reinforce Barron's (2000) argument that adults do not give youth the opportunity to speak on matters that affect them.

The Meanness Experts

While the girls were not convinced that girls' meanness is a form of bullying or aggression, as adults have conceptualized it, this is not to say that the issue is not a prevalent one in the lives of girls. Every girl had a story to share concerning girls' meanness, whether it involved a friend's betrayal or a nasty rumour. In offering their own personal narratives of this behaviour, one girl commented, "Sometimes your friends can be your worst enemies." They shared stories such as:

> I have like a guestbook on my website and one of my friends, they wrote something bad on it. Like she hasn't said anything bad about me yet, except for writing that, but she really gets along with me, but I don't know why she would write that on my guestbook. She was my friend. Her friend Jessica doesn't like me 'cause I go out with this guy she doesn't like, but we're cool now, but she told Krista that and Krista didn't know that she was fine with me, so now Krista hates me because Jessica hates me and Jessica doesn't even hate me anymore.

These narratives indicate several things about girls' aggression. First, it seems that girls will sometimes filter their meanness through other individuals or secondary sources, like a computer, thereby avoiding direct confrontation. This indicates that girls do not want to be perceived as mean. Second, girls themselves may have difficulty deciphering girls' mean behaviour. Lastly, these comments indicate that girls' status as "friends" can change regularly.

The girls were quick to identify and decipher the girls' mean behaviour in the video clips. After viewing the clip where three girls are spying on their friend Vanessa while she is talking to a boy whom one of the girls likes, the girls commented, "They're probably trying to hear stuff about her and then they're probably going to use it against her." The girls viewed a clip further along in the video where the same group of girls sees Vanessa talking to the boy again, after which they proceed to ignore Vanessa when she tries to catch up to them. The girls explained, "Well, the leader, she's all mad because she was jealous that he was flirting with her and she just kept on walking by." Clearly, the girls thought that meanness is often motivated by jealousy surrounding boys. Over all, the narratives shared by the girls, as well as the girls' familiarity with the behaviour in the video clips, suggest that girls are experts in the politics of girls' meanness.

It's All Part of Being a Girl

Undeniably, the girls viewed this mean behaviour as hurtful. One girl commented, "Like sometimes the stuff that hurts you is not always someone punching you but someone making fun of you." Yet, despite such comments as this and the numerous stories they shared, many of the girls concluded, "I think it is nature doing its course," "A lot of girls talk about girls" and "That's just what girls do," suggesting that meanness is just a part of growing up as a girl, as indicated by Phillips (2003) and Remillard and Lamb (2005). In fact, the girls offered specific ways in which a girl should react to meanness, saying "You can't get upset because then they'll just laugh at you and keep picking at you" and "If you tell the principal they can just make fun of you more… and they say that you're a tattle tale." Another girl, when asked if talking to an adult would help, replied, "It would stay the same probably." Yet another girl claimed that there was even a rule about not getting adults involved:

> This is sort of the rule for like… boys too but if, I don't know, it might be a bigger rule to girls but like if you get in a fight and like you don't think it's that big and you just wanna like stop fighting, you don't have to bring a teacher into it unless it gets really bad or a peer mediator.

The girls viewed a clip from the documentary *It's a Girl's World*, where Rachel Simmons, a leading "expert" on relational aggression sits down to talk with a group of girls about meanness. After seeing this clip the girls were asked what they thought of it. One girl argued, "Well I didn't agree with that lady who said talk to them and tell them your feelings because I don't agree with her at all, because if I tell her my feelings she will probably just think you're stupid." Other girls agreed with this statement, "They'll think you're a wussy" and "If you tell someone your feelings and they're the one who bullied you, they're just going to say 'yeah whatever' and that's happened to me before, 'cause I tend to get bullied sometimes and I tell like my best friends." Interestingly, another girl attacked this girl's comment, arguing, "It's not bullying!" Ultimately, there was a feeling of hopelessness conveyed by the girls about how to deal with girls' meanness, indicating that they view it as a permanent aspect of girlhood. Even after sharing all their stories, several girls went on to downplay girls' meanness, claiming that "Girls are different than boys, girls take like an hour to get over a fight and then they're best friends again." One girl tries to put girls' meanness into perspective, arguing,

> They're trying to be good, but they just can't and they're overflowing so to them they're just suppose to be mean and to the teachers, they're suppose to be good, so they're good in class...

This statement suggests that meanness may serve an important purpose in some girls' lives, allowing them to release their frustrations and cope with everyday life in girl world. Recognizing the role that meanness can play, it is safe to assume that the "problem" of so-called "girl bullying" cannot be addressed until girls are provided with an alternate, and presumably more empowering, avenue through which to negotiate their status as well as to release their anger and aggression.

It's Easy Being Mean

According to the girls, physical fights are "stupid" and "pointless"; thus, girls try to avoid these types of confrontations because "They don't want to get in trouble." One girl explains why girls do not usually have physical fights, "Because they don't really want to fight because if they pick a fight with the wrong person then they're gonna get hurt so they usually just do an emotional one like calling someone a loser or if they're like new to a school or something like that and then they'll call them new." Another girl claimed that girls tend not to fight because "It's easier to gossip and stuff." One girl wrote in her journal,

> I find being a gril [girl] is so so but as everybody dose [does] we have are [our] days. We get bullyed a lot but some of us are strong and some of us are weak. It all runs in the life of being a gril [girl]. We shouldn't be treated weather [whether] were [we're] Black or white, skinny or fat or the way we dress.

This statement suggests that girls' meanness is perceived as a part of being a girl, and some girls are able to adapt to it more than others. In other words, girls must learn to suffer through the judgments that they receive concerning their skin colour, weight and clothing. Perhaps meanness acts as a defence mechanism against these constant judgments, in that girls are able to divert the attention off themselves and onto other girls.

Popularity

According to the girls, meanness is very much a statement of popularity. When asked what makes a girl popular, the girls cited such things as:

> If you're richer than someone, if you live in a better house,
> Being older,
> They have better clothes,
> More money,
> They're skinny and perfect,
> Cheerleaders,
> They have a cute boyfriend,
> They're mean,
> Better at comebacks,
> Really pretty,
> Cute little purses,
> Being saucy,
> Their shape,
> Their hair's nice,
> They get what they want,
> They have their own table reserved for them,
> They have to be perfect.

The girls cited such things as "makeup," "jewellery," "boys." "being rude," "rumours" and "getting everything they want" as being important to popular girls. Some of these items are reminiscent of Bettie's (2003) discussion of "gender-specific commodities" that are used as markers of status among different groups of girls. One of the girls even contended that "Popularity is everything!" Describing the girls in the film *Odd Girl Out*, the girls made comments like "they're popular and they're mean."

On the contrary, girls who are unpopular were perceived in a particular way: "They're unnoticed and they're outsiders and it's just one of those people that sort of dresses… I don't know, and nobody notices them," "They're not as pretty," "They can have really bushy hair and big thick glasses" and "They don't get much power." One girl commented, "If you're not pretty, you're odd, dumb, stupid, stuff like that."

One girl recalled an incident where a girl propositioned her about becoming popular:

> A girl came up to me and gave me a piece of paper and she's like "do you wanna be popular?" and I'm like "I'm fine the way I am." She gave me it anyways and she said "learn it and if you wanna be popular come" and I'm like "where?" and "just come, you'll see me in the hallway." I'm like "why?" "You wanna be popular don't you?" "No, I just wanna be with my friends." "Oh okay then, go if you like, have a bad life."

Indeed, this illustrates that being popular is a status that is awarded only to select individuals. While it may be a status to which many girls aspire, there are specific rules that one must follow in order to be part of this elite. Certainly, this demonstrates the exclusivity that popularity holds in girl culture.

Rich, Pretty and Mean

According to the girls, popularity is awarded to rich girls who can afford the newest fashions and name-brand clothing. The girls indicated that if a girl is not rich she might still have a chance at being popular as long as she is pretty. One thing that the girls stressed about popular girls is that they are always mean, because that is how they maintain their place at the top. One girl argued, "You can't be mean unless you're pretty."

The girls agreed that there is always a leader in every girl group: she is usually the one who is physically positioned in the middle of the other girls and more importantly, the leader is always the rudest and meanest girl in the group. In relation to popularity, one girl wrote in her journal,

> I think it is fun but hard (talking about being a girl) 'cause you're juged [judged] by how you look and think and girls are always trying to be popular but it would be fun to swich [switch] bodys [bodies] for a day and see what they think about. But it's okay being a girl.

This statement suggests that while there may be perks to being a girl, girls are subject to constant criticism. The above comment also indicates that not only are girls judged on their appearance and peer status but that girls' thoughts are also being monitored and controlled. Her remarks, in particular, also suggest that unpopular girls are curious about the popular girl and would like to find out whether or not being popular would alleviate the judgments or eliminate insecurities.

Survival of the Meanest

The girls indicated that hierarchies among girls are reinforced through so-called relational aggression tactics, where acts of gossip, meanness and social alienation could secure a girl's status. Membership within particular groups is sometimes restricted.

As well, the girls indicated that popular girls maintain their popularity through being mean because "They make up rumours about people if you don't do what they say," and by "Whispering in people's ears and talking about you" and also "If they know something about this person that's bad or possibly can turn two people into a fight they'll go spread it and make everyone hate you." This lends support to the findings made by Merten (1997), Phillips (2003), Rose, Swenson and Walker (2004) and Cillessen and Mayeux (2004) concerning the relationship between popularity and girls' meanness. These tactics of meanness seem to provide tools for survival through which girls can negotiate their status among other girls. It would appear that girls' only resource is femininity. Therefore, some girls are able to "get ahead" by being mean.

Popularity is Power

When asked, "what is power?" the girls' responses included such things as, "Having control over people," "Being on an upper level," "Looks are power" and "Being nice to people... sometimes getting a lot of attention." The majority of the girls clearly indicated that popularity is synonymous with having power, stating, "If someone popular asks you to do something, you do it because they have power," "Popular people are powerful," "The more mean someone is, the more fear they [other people] have and it makes them more powerful 'cause they know they can do it to almost everyone" and "The more power to do it over and over and over to people." These remarks are consistent with Lease, Kennedy and Axelrod's (2002) finding that popularity is a key determinant of social power as well as with Currie and Kelly's (2006) analysis of the gendered economy.

  While the girls felt that, overall, those who are most powerful in their lives are adults (parents and teachers), in their peer world, popular girls possess the most power. Thus, being powerful was perceived by the girls as something that only popular girls get to experience, and as the girls indicated, there is only a small group of popular girls in every school. The rest of the girls, as one girl put it, "They just stand behind the shadows, hoping the popular girls don't notice them." The girls felt that popular girls take their frustrations out on other girls "Because they feel they have power over everyone... and they like to control people," and "They think it's cool." Seemingly, power is not something that was readily accessible to these girls, and even when girls are thought of as powerful, it is equated through such things as popularity (which is, for girls, largely weighed through material consumption and appearance). For instance, one girl concluded, "For the other people, what makes them not powerful is [being] ugly, fat, poor," suggesting that power is allocated to those girls who are pretty, skinny and rich, as suggested by Lease, Kennedy and Axelrod (2002) and Currie and Kelly (2006). Thus, girl power is superficially located within feminine standards of beauty.

The "Food Chain"

During discussions of power, the girls seemed well aware of social hierarchies. In reference to the videos, the girls identified power imbalances between groups without hesitation. For instance, when the girls were asked why the group of popular girls in *Odd Girl Out* were being mean to another girl, they responded as follows: "'Cause they don't like her," "Because they think she's a nerd," "And they think she's poor," "And they didn't get the chance to know who she actually was… so they don't know," "I think that group of girls is popular," and "Yeah they're popular and she's a geek."

One of the girls proudly cited a specific model of hierarchy referred to as the "food chain," stating,

> Jocks and cheerleaders, they're like at the top of the food chain. Like here's the food chain, jocks and cheerleaders, popular kids, and then there's us, and then there's unpopular kids, and then there's nerds, dorks, geeks. I memorized it.

This "food chain" model of school hierarchies is reflective of Phillips' (2003) discussion of the pecking order of youth. All the girls seem to rely on this model in terms of its status categories, attempting to situate themselves somewhere "in the middle," not quite popular but not unpopular either.

The Rules of the Ruling Class

In relation to the discussion of popularity, several of the girls stated that there is "A Popular Kid Code of Honour" which entailed rules such as, "Always sass everyone, always threaten people and meet them at the mall and threaten them," "If someone's in your way, push them," "Talk rude about others," "Get boys to like you," "And make sure the boys don't know about the things you say to the girls," and "whenever you have a chance to make fun of someone else you do." In addition to these rules, the girls also referred to status "codes," employed by popular girls in particular, where one girl claimed,

> Sometimes like if somebody's wearing something that's like not cool and someone is wearing something and they are cool, they might be saying, "I'm richer than you are and I can afford to buy good clothes and you can't."

This suggests that girls' own hierarchical system, based largely on appearance, is influenced by adults' socio-economic class structure. More specifically, girls who come from wealthy families have the resources to gain status through material consumption. Therefore, it would seem that girls are affected by conventional social class categories to the extent that coming from a working-class or middle-class background has important implications for how effectively a girl can negotiate her power among her peers.

The Boyfriend Rule

While the girls knew of the specific rules guiding popular girls, they also cited a certain rule intended for all girls, regardless of their social status:

> Sarah: I know a rule, at [school's name], it's definitely, if you break up with someone, okay... say I go out with... Zach.
> Natalie: Baker?
> Sarah: NO, NO, NO... I would never go out with him... Okay I go out with Zach, right... he broke up with me and I was crying... [says to Natalie] I was, right?! [Natalie nods]... I was really upset about it 'cause I really liked him and then Kaylee went over and asked him out and I wasn't over it — NEVER ASK A GUY OUT IF...
> Natalie: That's not a rule at [school's name]!!!
> Sarah: IT IS TO A LOT OF PEOPLE!! If a guy dumps a girl and the girl's not over it, ask permission for her to ask... er... if you ask him out...

Another girl reiterated this "rule" in another focus group, claiming, "Say I broke up with my boyfriend, and she wanted to go out with him, she can't, that's like the kinda rules they have."

Boy Crazy

Not only was being pretty a measure of a girl's power, so was being someone's girlfriend. Talking with the girls, it was evident that the higher-status girls were boy-defined. Yet, it seemed that the time invested in "chasing boys" (as some adults at the organization referred to it) was not in vain and should not be trivialized. According to the girls, being the subject of male desire was a source of power that seems to have no other equivalent in girl culture.

When asked, "what do you think is the best thing about being a girl?" some of the girls responded with,

> Sarah: BOY friends!
> Lindsay: Yeah having boyfriends.
> Sarah: 'Cause they're so hot.

At the age of ten, some of these girls claimed to have had multiple "boy-friends":

> Sarah: I've had three boyfriends in one day.
> Melanie: Well, she [speaking about Lindsay] had boyfriends back in grade one.

Sarah: I only started having boyfriends in grade two and I've had thirty-two!
Natalie: I started in grade primary.

While the lower-status girls mentioned boys they liked, they did not show the same intense interest in boyfriends that was exhibited by some of the higher-status girls. However, one shy, lower-status girl attempted to legitimize girls' emphasis on boys, stating, "mostly all girls are into boys," suggesting that perhaps having a boyfriend, or at least a crush, is an important aspect of girlhood. Yet, the higher-status girls seemed to actively participate in the pursuit of male attention and boyfriends, while the lower-status girls seemed quite passive in this pursuit. Presumably, this difference could be explained by the higher-status girls possessing "desirable" feminine qualities that made them appealing to boys. This finding supports Currie and Kelly's (2006) argument that maintaining boys' attention is a source of power for girls.

White on Top

One final, but important aspect of popularity and status that was identified by the girls was racial hierarchies. After being shown the clip from *Odd Girl Out*, where a group of girls tells another girl that she is sitting at their table and she has to leave, the girls were asked why they thought that girl was not allowed to sit with them. The girls offered responses that were similar, stating, "No offence but they might not like her because of her colour" and "Maybe because she might be new or 'cause she has different colour skin." One girl claimed, "Maybe they thought that if they sat with her or something, it would ruin their image," indicating that perhaps a girl's race or ethnicity could determine her status among peers. This supports Bettie's (2003) research finding that the girls viewed "whiteness" as the privileged position.

Male Privilege and the Power of Action

The power possessed by popular girls was sharply contrasted with the power exuded by boys and men. When asked how boys and men show their power, the girls responses' included, "By fighting," "By bullying their girlfriends or whatever," "Guys do like a strut," "They fight," "How much muscle they have," "They join the football team and then they think they're popular" and "Drinking." Several of the girls thought that boys' and girls' power is equal, while a few of the girls said that "Girls are way more powerful" because "There's more girls on this planet" and "Girls live longer than boys do." At the same time, they argued that, "But boys can fight and kill people," "Boys can buy knives" and "Boys' power is killing power, girls' power is threatening power." Ultimately, they concluded that, "Boys' power is a lot different than girls' power." Overall, most of girls felt that boys and men were more powerful than girls and women. One girl claimed, "I think guys just think they are [more powerful]." Another girl stated, "Boys are more powerful because of their actions" and "It's like if you're not going my way, I'm gonna hit ya." The girls in that particular focus group agreed with this statement. Yet, in reference to their own lives, several of the girls felt that women (their mothers) had more spending power when it came to shopping for the family, which supports the work of Griffin (2004). Yet, in other instances, they thought that men, whether it was a father, step-father, or a boyfriend of their mothers, often made the more important decisions, which concerned things such as money.

Social Injustices in Girlhood

The girls revealed four major social injustices that they endure on a day-to-day basis:

- problems with authority figures in relation to abuse of power and rule enforcement;
- sexual harassment;
- physical abuse by boys; and
- racism and discrimination.

Illustrating the first social injustice, one girl shared her story about one adult's abuse of power:

> We were going to play truth or dare, the [adult] leader told us not to play truth or dare — we decided not to- — he told us to get out of the corner — we went in another corner, where he sat there and watched us so he said we could sit there as long as he could watch us. We decided we weren't going to sit there anymore and we sat out on the playground. He sent people to spy on us and then that one person told that one person and they told the leader and then the leader told us and he said "you can go to the office or you can sit right there" and so we chose to sit right there and then we told all the people and we said "ya know let's choose the office so we can go tell [director] and [female leader] what happened." Then I said to him "ya know what, we choose the office" so we went up to the office and we were sitting there and he decided to follow us and he got his witnesses, which were actually lying because it wasn't true... and so the leader was trying to get us suspended!! Female leaders know what it's like to be a girl as long as they're not like stupid and guy leaders don't know what it's like to be a girl and you know why they took my side? 'cause the boss of the whole thing saw how mad I was in my eyes and that I was about to cry, I was so mad that people

were lying. [Female leader] saw in my eyes that I was going to cry and actually did afterwards...

It was also apparent from my observations of the girls' interactions with the staff at the organizations that many of girls felt restricted and constrained by a multitude of rules readily enforced by the adults in their lives. Seemingly, they were constantly being watched. Evidently, the rules that the girls appeared to resent the most were the ones that controlled what they could wear. They also identified a sexual double standard regarding this rule. For instance, according to the girls:

> Sasha: You're not allowed to wear short shirts and tank tops and stuff like that.
> Lindsay: It's because guys or girls will make fun of you if you're flat or something.
> Sasha: What's that mean?
> Sarah: You have no chest.
> Sasha: Girls aren't allowed to wear shorts either... except long shorts or capris but guys are allowed and they wear muscle shirts all the time and we're not allowed tank tops.

Although all the girls seemed to oppose this rule, they were quite compliant even in circumstances where defiance might be warranted. For instance, during one of the focus group sessions, it was an incredibly warm day and one girl would not remove the shirt she was wearing over a tank top, as she did not want to be penalized. However, some of the higher-status girls pushed the envelope with this rule. Some of the girls wore tank tops and short skirts in all situations where they thought this rule would not be enforced. One girl even insisted on wearing just her bra as a top during the final session, despite the male janitor being readily present in the building. While rules governing the girls' femininity and, in this case, what the girls could wear was apparent at both research locations, they seemed more readily enforced at the location with more minority girls. Certainly, this suggests that adults may monitor minority girls' femininity more closely than that of white girls. However, it is also possible that this was just a difference of organizational structures. Indeed, the important finding here is that young girls are subject to specific rules that govern their sexuality and feminine appearance.

Being teased about having a flat chest introduces the second social injustice suffered by girls, sexual harassment. One such incident was highlighted in a comment made by Lindsay:

> Lindsay: I have a shirt like that, you know my pink and brown and white one that goes like this but it comes down like this, they make fun of me in that. You don't have to have chests for those shirts, it's the design of

those shirts and they always make fun of me.
Researcher: Who makes fun of you?
Lindsay: Shane and he's the leader and he's a boy.

Another girl, responding to what she thinks is the worst thing about being a girl stated, "I think the worst thing is being at home with your mom and dad, your dad makes fun of you for wearing a bra and snaps your bra strap." Ultimately, this sparked a discussion among the girls about boys in their school continually snapping their bra straps. Surprisingly, the girls do not seem to view these incidences as "harassment"; rather they are seen as general annoyances in their lives.

A third social injustice discussed by the girls was the frequency of cross-gender bullying and more specifically, boys physically harassing girls. Equally problematic is the way in which adults respond to this behaviour. For instance, one girl shares her story:

Tara: I was just sitting and for no reason some guy and girl they come running along and one guy he just like kicks rocks at me.
Sabrina: He what?
Tara: He kicks rocks at me and so I went and I told the monitor and she went over to him and he's like "well she called me fat" and whatever and I... "well no I didn't" and so the monitor sends us in to the principal and he knows that I didn't do that so he'll say "well.... why don't you... we just say sorry and we won't have to do this" and I'm like "yeah whatever" so he says sorry and he goes outside and then my friends and his friends are together so we went back to hang with our friends and they're like "what happened?" and we said "well he just says sorry" and he's just like "why didn't you guys do that here?" and then later one of his friends who is one of my brother's friends 'cause he lives in our neighbourhood and he came up to me and he's like "Chris was lying about you calling him fat" and I was like "I know."
Tara: 'Cause boys...
Chloe: Think they're more superior.
Taylor: 'Cause they're think they're better so they call them names so if the boys call the girls names it makes them feel bigger. Like one guy he's making fun of me and I went home and I told my mom and she told me that he just likes me and if he calls me that again just tell him that I know he likes me and he can stop doing that, and I did that and he stopped making fun of me.

Another girl shares her experiences with boys' aggression:

Mia: Yes, 'cause the little boy, Tyson, today he whomped me in the face 'cause he slapped me so hard.
Keisha: I know, he's so rude.

In addition, another girl explained that, "Some boys have nails and they dig their nails into your head." The prevalence of these narratives suggests that boys' aggression toward girls is equally problematic for girls' as is "relational aggression" from other girls, if not more so.

Some girls have learned to match the physical aggression exhibited by boys, as exemplified in the following discussion:

> Researcher: So boys hurt girls sometimes?
> Krista: Uh huh, like today...
> Jennifer: ...and I was like "do do do" and my hand accidentally when by his...
> Melissa: You were chasing him, what are you talking about??
> Jennifer: There's this older boy named Michael, he's right weird and everything... I was like "Marshall give it back!"
> Krista: And plus she does the pressure point if he doesn't give it back.
> Jennifer: What I do is... I did this... if you do this, the two nerves in your neck on either side — if you pinch those nerves then it really hurts — watch (demonstrates on Melissa).
> Melissa: OWWWWW.
> [Girls laugh]
> Researcher: And does that show him that you're more powerful than him?
> Jennifer: Uh huh... if he takes something of mine I'll show him, I'm gonna go haywire... I give him the pressure point and he'll drop whatever he has.
> Krista: The only time I do that is when I'm angry.
> Jennifer: I only do it when he takes something of mine.
> Melissa: I'll either yell really loud...
> Krista: Like today we were playing this kind of game and Melissa said my name, "Krista, go get the ball!" and Mark and the other guys went, and I was like "Is your name Krista?" and he's like "Yeah!" and I yelled "Is your name Krista?"

The final social injustice highlighted by the minority girls is racism and discrimination, yet many of the white girls denied its existence. Initially, the girls were all quite hesitant to even talk about race and ethnicity, suggesting that it is perhaps viewed as a taboo. When asked about racism, several of the higher-status, white girls adamantly stated that: "Yeah, no, no... not in our school anyhow! There's no racism!" and "We have no racism!" Other white girls were also unaware of how minority girls can be treated differently. For instance:

> Researcher: Do you think girls with different colour skin from you get treated differently?
> Amy: Some
> Researcher: Do you have any idea how racism affects how girls are treated?

Amy: No.
Melissa: No.

Yet, as the discussion progressed, several of the white girls recalled this incident:

Natalie: There's a grade six. There's a grade six and she was wearing pajamas pants and so was Sarah, and Mr. Clancy [the principal] came and talked to her and not Sarah.
Sarah: And she was Black! Yeah he went and talked to her about wearing pajamas pants and didn't even come to me.
Natalie: Yeah! And you walked past him.
Heidi: No, 'cause Mr. Clancy is white and he understands white people and he doesn't understand Black people.
Sarah: I walked past him so many times!

However, it appeared for many of the white girls, regardless of their socio-economic background, that racism was not an issue "around here." For example, one girl argued, "Like back in the day there would be more racism down there" (Southern United States).

When asked whether they thought a girl's race or culture brought about different experiences, one white girl responded, "No, because every time you watch them walk into school they're just the same as everybody else. I don't think they have any different experiences." In the midst of our discussion, another white girl asked, "Say you have Black skin, can you like get a different colour skin?" indicating that she was unaware of the social circumstances of racial and ethnic minorities beyond their physiological differences. Seemingly, white privilege prohibits these girls from acknowledging the social injustices suffered by ethnic minorities. One could speculate that racism programs such as Stop Racism that teach children not to see skin colour and treat everyone the same have produced the "we're all the same" attitude exemplified in the girls' responses. Regardless of why these girls denied minority girls' experiences with racism and discrimination, their lack of knowledge concerning race was apparent.

The minority girls in my groups shared entirely different narratives of racism and discrimination:

Researcher: So today we're going to talk about race
Keisha: Oh.
Mia: Like white people making fun of Black people and stuff.
Salena: I don't like racist people, I'm sorry but I have to tell you this, you know how I told you that my vice principal is sick, right...
Researcher: Yeah.
Salena: And um, the gym teacher plays as the vice principal sometimes — he's really responsible [said sarcastically] so he's doing that and we

have this really really rude gym teacher named Mr. Walsh, and when like, me and my friends sat down 'cause we were tired and he said "Look at you guys, what a bunch of cry babies you guys are," right, and when um, when we came to get tennis rackets for recess and lunch, and um we said "Mr. Walsh can we use some tennis rackets?" He's like "no" and we're like "okay" and then we come, we come, we go to the bins, 'cause there's bins but they were all out like they were outside and yeah he was just really rude.

Mia: I thought that had something to do with racist.

Salena: Oh yeah… in gym class, sorry, in gym class right…

Researcher: So is he a white teacher?

[Girls nod their heads]

Salena: In gym class, me and my friend were both kinda… and um, we're cousins and um we were playing and we were playing and we got out and um and we got out and then he's like "look at you guys" and this is the same with my music teacher but she's the same colour as us and she's like, she's like we were playing basketball today in music and she's like — she was just letting us play on our own the coloured people, right and the rest of the people that she let play she was like directing it and everything, she wouldn't even show us how to play.

Researcher: So do you think you get treated differently because you're coloured? By teachers?

Salena: Yeah…

Mia: Oh, one girl, Tamara she called me a nigger before…

Molly: Oh my God you should never say that!

Mia: I know but… I told her that two wrongs don't make a right or something like that I told her and then I just started walking home and then one day I asked her to play and she said I don't play with "black-stabbers" instead of backstabbers, that was so rude.

Aaliyah: Um… someone at my school…

Molly: Amanda?

Aaliyah: Rachel…

Molly: Oh.

Aaliyah: Rachel yeah she was talking racist and saying that Black people shouldn't go around white people and… saying the N word to everyone.

Another group was asked "Do you think the colour of a girl's skin affects how others treat her?" Chloe, the only minority girl in that particular group, responded "Yeah, especially if you have bushy hair. Like people call me Afro woman." These stories shared by the minority girls in my sessions indicate that racism and discrimination is a prevalent part of their everyday lives despite the efforts put forth by the white girls to deny it.

The Best Thing about Being a Girl

At the end of the final sessions with the girls, they were asked, "what is the best thing about being a girl?" After careful thought and deliberation, the girls indicated contentment in engaging in feminine activities such as sleepovers, putting on make-up and shopping. The girls elaborate:

> You can wear skirts
> Um… you can wear make-up, you can wear mini-skirts, and tank tops…
> You can go shopping at girl stores
> The things that you can do and wear
> Paint your nails
> Like… yeah you can talk about boys and have slumber parties

Some of the girls' responses to the question were not as reflective of being a "girl" and, instead, highlighted things that girls get to do when they grow up:

> Heidi: When you grow up, you get your mom, or grandmother, either takes you out to the club to go drinking and you get drunk.
> Sarah: And ya know the best part about being a girl is that you get to grow up and be in labour and go (lets out a big grunt).
> [Girls laugh]
> Sarah: And then you have a cute little baby, and the mom's best part is…
> Natalie: Names.
> Sarah: Naming the baby.
> Natalie: Oh my God, you so took my thing.
> Sarah: Yeah she did, so um because the moms do all the work, the hard work, the messy kinda hard work and she has to go through the labour and her water breaking… (girls giggling in the background) and the pregnancy.
> Heidi: And people calling her fat.
> Sarah: 'Cause she has a baby in her stomach and it goes Bomp Bomp Bomp.
> Heidi: And sticking a hand up there.
> Sarah: I don't want a hand up my rear end… my stomach… then you get to name it and I am naming my kid Paris and I'm naming a guy Jake 'cause I love that name and a girl I'm naming Allie and I'm not naming it Alison, I'm naming it Allie.

In talking about mothering and naming babies, the girls became extremely animated. One of the most important things to these girls appeared to be motherhood. Even though they were quite disgusted by the thought of entering puberty and having sex to get pregnant, they appeared enchanted by the prospect of one day having babies. The girls illustrate this point:

Sarah: I'd rather get it over with [puberty]... I'm not saying this in a sick way but I want to have kids.
Natalie: Me too.
Sarah: Like I don't mean I want to have sex... I want to have kids...
Natalie: I think that would be so cool to hold a baby and the names are the best.
Sarah: Yeah.
Lindsay: But it's hard to name them.
Natalie: I already got a whole bunch of names.
Lindsay: Paris is one.
Natalie: Yeah.
Sarah: Marry someone with the last name Hilton.

Evidently, these girls are anxiously awaiting womanhood as it promises to be something better than that which is offered in girlhood. Not only are girls waiting to become women, they are also waiting to have "power."

Conclusion

Arising from these findings are themes related to popularity and power. First and foremost, the girls offered a different perspective of girls' so-called meanness than is offered by most adults. More specifically, the girls seemed to present meanness as a perpetual and prevalent issue in girl culture. As well, the girls' seemed to normalize meanness, suggesting that it is an accepted feature of girlhood and that it serves as an exclusive avenue whereby some girls are able to release their anger and aggression.

In relation to my specific research questions concerning girl aggression, the girls' indicated that hidden forms of aggression, namely meanness, are more common among popular higher-status girls; yet, the girls also suggested that girls engage in meanness to varying degrees, independent of their race, ethnicity, class or peer status. In other words, meanness is not related exclusively to popularity and higher status. The girls indicated that there are personal as well as social benefits to using hidden forms of aggression. They claimed that it is easier and more acceptable for girls to be mean than to be physically aggressive, as the latter could ultimately lead to social rejection.

A key finding in my research is that popularity implies power, meaning that the girls' perceived popularity as an exclusive means of power for girls. It appeared that girls were quite conscious of their status among other girls, and most attempted to position themselves in the middle between the powerful and the marginalized. Although all girls are subject to some rules related to feminine appearance, behaviour and interactions with boys, it seemed that popular girls were inundated with such rules. This suggests that girls with power are carefully governed. Furthermore, the girls identified distinct gender differences in relation to power, where women are powerful with words and men are powerful with actions. Most importantly, the girls indicated that girls' power is heavily constrained by structures of gender, race and class, where the criteria for being powerful is prettiness, whiteness and wealth. The girls also suggested that power is allocated to girls who can capture the attention of boys without presenting themselves as too sexual. Seemingly, meanness provides girls with a way of negotiating and maintaining their power among the powerless. Thus, meanness is also a testament to girls' resiliency amidst oppressive forces. The girls' narratives surrounding adults' abuse of authority, sexual and physical harassment by men and boys and racial discrimination, as well as the girls' anticipation of womanhood, further demonstrate girls' powerlessness in society.

The girls' responses to my questions regarding power indicated that feelings of powerlessness are reflective of girls' suppression of aggression, whereas girls with power are able to express their aggression, through meanness, to reaffirm their higher status. For the girls in my study, power represented popularity, which, in turn, was constrained by structures of race, class and gender. The girls did not associate female power with physical force; this was the purview of men. For girls, power is something that must be negotiated passively or at least covertly. Accordingly, it would seem that girls' power is real in the sense that it has significant meaning in their lives; however, the sad irony is that girls' power has very little social or political consequence beyond "girl world." It would seem that girls' power is inevitably constrained by structures of patriarchy, class and race, and, thus, it is not something that is readily located within girlhood. Instead, powerful girls are those who quietly negotiate their position.

Chapter Five

Race, Class and Gender

This chapter outlines themes from the girls' discussions related to hierarchies of gender, race and class. I discuss the implications of these structures on what girls are taught about aggression and, in turn, how girls' express their anger and aggression. The chapter revisits the girls' perceptions of meanness and violence, revealing important gendered, racialized and classed versions of girls' aggression. In addition, the girls' views of feminine stereotypes such as the "good girl" and the "bad girl" are examined, as are the "types" of girls who subscribe to these standards. The girls' narratives surrounding girlfighting and what these narratives suggest about girls' negotiations of femininity are also explored.

Girls' Anger

When I asked the girls how they deal with anger, they offered responses indicating that girls often conceal their anger from others through such things as gossip, breaking something or crying. For instance, they stated:

> Lindsay: OH MY GOD! That girl was so mean to me... and then they spread gossip... They go like "hi" — oh hi were you talking about me — pouf! [Punches the air]
> Krista: Like go to the bathroom and like... handle it and break something.
> Melissa: Cry.
> Jennifer: Go to the bathroom and break something.
> Nicola: Scream into a pillow.
> Ariel: Or they could just go tell someone...
> Natalie: Cry.

The girls also provided personal accounts of how they deal with their anger. Most indicated that they internalize or hide their frustrations from others; some of the girls revealed that they would direct their anger toward an individual or object. Only one girl, who was white, said she uses physical force. For example, the girls stated:

> Melissa: If I'm at home, I'll scream in my pillow and then when I feel better I'll come out.
> Jennifer: I bang my head on the wall.
> Krista: I'd wait til my mom comes in with pizza.

Melissa: Usually when I feel bad I slam down my bag, I go to my room and I just wait until my mom comes in with something that I want or something like maybe a hug or something to make me feel better.

Amy: The only two places that I ever cry is on my sofa or on my bed, those are the only two places that I'll actually cry.

Melissa: I cry on my mom's shoulder.

Jennifer: I don't like my mom trying to find me so whenever I'm angry I shut — I slam the door shut, my bedroom, I slam my door and then I just go in my room and hide under my bed.

Nicola: I would yell in a pillow.

Ariel: Yeah, put a dartboard up and put their school picture up and start throwing darts at it.

Nicola: I draw a picture of them and I throw a basketball at it.

Melanie: I just make faces.

Sarah: I take it and then I talk about them behind their back... (raises her voice — addresses Natasha) I didn't talk about you behind your back, I talked about Jade! And you don't know me well enough to know that I was trying to get it out of Kaitlyn... I don't cry in front of people, unless my feelings really got hurt.

Selena: If I get mad, and I'm outside, right, and I'm playing skipping — all I do is swing really fast.

Keisha: When I get mad I push somebody.

All the girls said that girls often hide their anger, which supports Crowley Jack (1993), Campbell (1993) and Brown's (2003) finding that girls are taught to suppress their anger. The girls also maintained that there are benefits to girls hiding their anger from other people. One girl said that the reason this happens is "so their friends won't get angry." Thus, most of the girls seem to indicate that girls avoid confrontations as much as possible, even in circumstances of severe frustration. The girls maintained that anger must be kept to a minimum and managed carefully. The girls exemplified these situations:

Sabrina: Say someone pushed you in front of the class, um... or corrected you or something and then uh...

Chloe: Or tripped you on the bus... that's happened to me a few times.

Sabrina: If you made a scene you'd get embarrassed like yeah... so I would just like roll my eyes and say "get a life girl!"

Ariel: Well, not say it out loud but...

Sabrina: Well... yeah...

Yet, many of the girls also agreed that popular girls are often the exception. They maintained that popular girls do not conceal their anger. The girls illustrate this argument in stating, "Popular girls probably show their anger and they get angry at one person, they either threaten them or they might say if you leave me alone I just might let you join," "They're mean and they're like 'Oh my God, I'm like so gonna kill that person,'" "I think they gossip," "They cross their hands and they go like that and push their hair," "Spread rumours," "Hurt people," "When they're angry they push people and be even more rude than you're supposed to be. They threaten to put pictures up online… and try to make them feel very bad," "Sometimes when they see someone with something that they hate they'll go 'oh I love that bracelet' and then they go [makes gagging noise] and then they'll start spreading rumours about it."

When asked to account for the different versions of girls' anger, where some girls outwardly express their anger and others do not, the girls indicated that most girls avoid fighting. For example, in response to the question, "So if a girl's mad why wouldn't she just go up and punch a girl?" the girls said:

> Natalie: I probably would.
> Lindsay: Detention!
> Sasha: 'Cause you get in trouble.
> Natalie: I punch guys, I don't punch girls.
> Lindsay: It's illegal to punch a girl.

The girls claimed that popular girls engage in talk fights when they are angry. Similarly, when asked, "what kinds of girls fight the most?" the girls unanimously stated that it was popular girls. Also, in relation to this, another group was asked, "So how come some girls express their anger verbally and some punch?" the girls responded:

> Keisha: Some girls are nice.
> Mia: Some girls argue.
> Aaliyah: Nice girls, like the ones that they dress up nice, they like to argue and um the girls that don't like to dress nice they like to fight.

Overall, the girls believed that girls' anger is significantly different from that of boys, in that girls might orally express their anger, while boys tend to engage in physical fights. When asked "How do you think girls show their anger differently (from boys)?" the girls replied:

> Aaliyah: Talking!
> Aaliyah: Yeah talk fights.
> Mia: Arguing.
> Selena: Yeah or giving the fist.

The girls also indicated that girls who express their anger physically are regarded as "bitches" who merely crave attention, suggesting that girls find it difficult to rationalize girls' overt expressions of anger. For instance, when asked, "What makes some girls want to go off and punch a girl or fight with her?" the girls claimed:

> Ariel: 'Cause they've held, held up their anger for too long and they just want to take it out on someone.
> Chloe: To get noticed.

The girls understood this variation in how girls express their anger in terms of what they are taught about aggression. According to the girls, some girls are taught, "Don't do it, if you do it you get disciplined," or maybe even, as Melissa put it: "like get angry, but don't get aggressive and don't get physical 'cause if you're angry, either just put your head down on your desk or like try and go somewhere else but don't try to hurt them or anything."

While the girls thought that some girls might express their anger "by fighting," all the girls in the study, independent of their racial, ethnic or class backgrounds, indicated that they tend to conceal their anger and frustration. This finding opposes Taylor, Gilligan and Sullivan's (1995) finding that minority girls are not socialized under the same constraints of anger as white, middle-class girls and Lamb's (2001) claim that middle-class girls feel the most pressure not to express their anger.

Girls' Perceptions of Girl Aggression and Violence

Most of the girls in the study thought that it was never completely acceptable for girls to engage in violent or aggressive behaviour. Most of the girls said that fighting can be necessary for girls in extenuating circumstances where a girl must defend herself or maybe even when she is involved in some sort of organized contact sport. For example:

> Chloe: Kinda like defend yourself from older siblings.
> Natalie: If somebody's trying to molest you then you can fight with them.
> Chloe: Boxing, wrestling.

The girls also believed that violence is more common among girls from "poorer families." They identified specific "Black neighbourhoods" in their area as more violent. One girl contended that violence and aggression in these "poor areas" is viewed as "just like a normal everyday thing and they get in fights." Natalie seemed proud that her father lives in one of these areas and that there was once a gang fight in the middle of the day. According to her, "Girls have to be more tougher to protect themselves" in these areas "'cause there's a whole bunch of boys and gangsters around." Other girls claimed that aggressive girls are "Girls who grow up with a lot of things happening" and "usually they're people that aren't well known and they want to be known for something like where they come from." Thus, violence and aggression was perceived as a necessity for minority girls living in conditions of poverty.

When the girls were shown the video clip involving a fight between a white girl and a Black girl and asked which girl they thought was more aggressive, the girls said it was the Black girl. This was the unanimous response, despite the fact that the fight between the two girls broke out after the white girl hit the Black girl in the head with a ball during a game of basketball. This suggests that Black girls are perceived as more aggressive than white girls, even by Black girls.

Most of the girls thought that girls of different ethnicities and racial backgrounds expressed aggression differently. This is contradictory to the views of many of the white girls, who also asserted that racial and ethnic minority girls do not have different experiences from white girls. Most of the girls also indicated that there is more pressure placed on white girls to not fight. A comment made by Natalie suggests that physical fighting is perhaps not a necessity for white girls:

> Natalie: Yeah, because white girls, no offence to white girls, but…
> Sarah: You are a white girl!!
> Natalie: I know, but they're usually rich and if they break a nail then they're gonna get like Oh my God!

The minority girls were reluctant at first to discuss race in relation to aggression, as they would begin to share something and then stop themselves. After indicating that "yes," there is difference between the behaviour of white girls and Black girls, the girls proceeded to respond to the question of how this behaviour is different but they were hesitant:

> Mia: Yeah, they're more like… never mind I was going to say something.
> Molly: You guys say something.
> Selena: I'm not saying anything…

Yet, once reassured that their opinions were all important, the girls elaborated on specific differences they thought existed in girls' aggression based on "race." They indicated that the aggression of Black girls is much more direct than that of white girls, which is reminiscent of the findings made by Simmons (2002), Chesney-Lind and Irwin (2004), and Ness (2004). For instance, the Black girls stated:

> Mia: I was going to say something… I'm not being rude but I don't know if it's bad or if it's not but… they're [Black girls] more like pissier and stuff.

> Selena: Some of my friends that are coloured, they're like really really pissy.
> Mia: Black girls handle it more as in fighting, but white girls are more arguing.
> Selena: Black people have more attitude than white people.

This same group of girls indicated that their behaviour is different from white girls because they are disadvantaged, at which point, Molly, the only white girl in the group, presented a challenge:

> Mia: Most Black people don't have as much as white people.
> Molly: Have much? Are you kidding? They... most of the time I think they're rich.
> Keisha: Oh?
> Molly: 'Cause they have way better clothes... seriously.
> Selena: Just because they have better clothes it doesn't mean that they're rich! Everybody knows how to shop!
> Mia: Every culture is different, like Black people have attitude.

Most of the other girls were not as forthcoming in the discussion of how or why they thought aggression is different for white and Black girls. However, they were all adamant that there are distinct variations. One white girl claimed, "They [Black girls] usually fight more and parents usually teach them a lot too." Another white girl suggested that Black girls tend to be more physically aggressive, while white girls are often more verbally aggressive. She stated:

> Melissa: For me... some Black girls are more [sighs] more physical than the white ones but the white ones are more like rude.

She went on to make the argument that white girls are "little angels" and insinuates that Black girls are not:

> Melissa: [referring to her school demographic] There's actually a lot more white girls than there is Black girls, but the Black girls are more rude and all that. Like the white girls are little angels but the Black ones are just not.

As far as providing a rationale for why they thought aggression was different for Black and white girls, it appeared as though the girls were drawing on cultural stereotypes to formulate their responses. They suggested, "Black people live in the hood I guess... in poor areas... which causes problems" and "Maybe they're mad because of the... uh... uh... slave thing." While the girls' understandings of how experiences of aggression may differ based on race, class and ethnic backgrounds were unsophisticated, their responses were nonetheless enlightened and thoughtful. For instance, the girls perceived violence and aggression as a necessity, at times, for marginalized girls living in conditions of poverty, racial oppression and/or violence.

Lessons in Aggression

While many of the girls believed that girls are taught to avoid physical confrontation, the minority girls offered a different perspective, in reporting that they were taught to use physical aggression when necessary. This supports the findings of Taylor, Gilligan and Sullivan (1995), Chesney-Lind and Shelden (1998), Flannery and Huff (1999), Lamb (2001), Simmons (2002), Chesney-Lind and Pasko (2004) and Bettie (2003). The girls stated:

> Mia: My friend Tamara... this girl named Niki... like she was going to beat up her sister... but my mom told me if someone is gonna beat up my sister... you're allowed to fight when you have to.
> Selena: My mom says that if someone hits you really hard, you should be able to hit them back, like defend yourself a lot.
> Mia: And you're good at that.
> Keisha: Yeah like my mom said, once this guy — this guy kicked me in the belly but I didn't kick him back, I started crying. Then my mom said whenever a guy kicks you, kick him back... [continues to mumble on]
> Molly: I'm not allowed to kick girls.
> Keisha: Like if one of your sisters accidentally hits this girl and then this girl says that she's going to gang your sister then you have to fight.
> Mia: If my sister gets herself in trouble, she'll fight herself.

Seemingly, these girls were taught and even encouraged by their families to use aggression in defending themselves or a sibling. Yet, contrary to Lamb (2001) it did not appear as though they were taught to wear their aggression with pride.

Policing Femininity

One prominent occurrence in all the sessions with the girls was a constant policing of other girls' behaviour and appearance, whether it was girls in the films or other girls in the groups. During the video clips the girls would make comments such as, "Oh... I like that top it's cute," "I don't like that skirt," "Oh... pretty clothes!" "They're pretty but they walk like they're all that!" "Whoa, so pretty!" "they're skinny and perfect," "That skirt is cute, I like it, it's pretty," "Yup... she's rude, she's snobby and she's just plain rude," "She thinks she's pretty," "She thinks she's popular," "She's pretty there," and "I think the girl in the blue shirt is pretty."

These comments evaluating other girls' femininity were often made in the context of stories. The girls would reference the behaviour of a particular girl to establish their point. In many cases, the same names would continually come up in the discussions. Evaluations of girls' appearance were especially common among the higher-status girls. These girls would often talk negatively about other girls in relation to their behaviour and feminine appearance, which is consistent with the research findings of Laidler and Hunt (2001) that popular girls frequently participate in the critiquing of other girls. This suggests that higher-status girls participate in relational aggressive behaviour such as gossip and social alienation more often than lower-status girls and supports the claims made by Simmons (2002), Chesney-Lind and Irwin (2004) and Ness (2004) that relational aggression is a middle-class issue.

Occasionally these lower-status girls would turn the feminine evaluations of appearance onto themselves. This supports Chesney-Lind and Shelden (1998) suggestion that working- and lower-class girls may not be able to measure up to the white, middle-class standard of beauty that is central to popularity. For instance, several of the girls made comments like "I'm ugly, don't look at me" and "I'm not very pretty."

According to the girls, not being pretty has serious repercussions. When asked, what happens when a girl is not pretty, the girls responded with, "They probably put on a bunch of makeup," "sometimes they hide their faces with plastic bags or something," "they can lose their popularity, they can't be popular" and "they can be an outsider." Thus, the girls placed a great deal of emphasis on a girl's appearance as a measure of her worth. They had even done this with me in the beginning of our sessions, commenting on my clothes and hairstyle, all of which seemed to measure up to their standard as they did tell me I was pretty.

Pretty Little White Girl

A recurring theme in the girls' discussions was the notion that whiteness is equated with beauty. After watching all the films depicting mean girls, the girls were asked why there were no minority girls represented. Their responses included such things as, "'Cause sometimes they just want the pretty girls and that's it!" and "'Cause they think they're [white girls] prettier." The minority girls were especially conscious of this beauty standard in relation to hair; Mia, a Black girl made the comment, "Some Black people don't have as nice hair as white people." Yet, Molly, a white girl opposed this argument, stating, "you can braid your hair and it will stay that way... mine will just come right out!" Yet, Aaliyah retaliated, "Your hair is smoother!!" suggesting that smooth (white) hair is more desirable. This finding supports Griffin's (2004) discussion of the racialized standards of beauty that promote smooth and glossy hair as opposed to so-called "nappy" hair.

Good Girls versus Bad Girls

During the focus group sessions, the girls were shown two images, one of a "good girl" and the other of a "bad girl," and asked what they thought of each girl. The girls' responses to the first image included the following: "She's good, she never gets in trouble, she's teacher's pet," "She's pretty," "She's smiling too hard," "She's kinda likeable," "She's not even overweight or chubby," "Always does everything to perfection," "Too smart," "She's nice, sweet, kind" and "popular." These comments ultimately encompassed all the traits that the girls felt a good girl should possess. Some of the higher-status girls, however, presented some hostility and resentment towards the good girl image. For instance, one higher-status, white girl stated, "She's a good girl and she's probably one of the people I'd never hang out with." Another white, higher-status girl stated, "I have to admit that that's the way stuff goes, nice people get last," to which another white, higher-status girl agreed, "I think that's unfair but that's how it goes."

On the other hand, the bad girl was believed to encompass everything from being "slutty," "doing the ho train," "dirty-dancing" (the middle-class girls proceeded to demonstrate how bad girls dance), to "They dye their hair when their mothers tell them not to, they drink, they smoke," "They wear skeleton earrings," "They wear camouflage and baggy pants," "Have lots of piercings and tattoos," and they engage in behaviour such as "breaking windows, stealing cars, setting off alarms, being rude." To the higher-status girls, being a bad girl was viewed as desirable, and they referred more to the bad girls' sexuality, which is consistent with Currie and Kelly's (2006) claim that femininity is largely gauged by sexuality. However, to most of the lower-status girls, bad girls were viewed as rebels who defy femininity by acting out in unfeminine ways. The girls were definitely divided in their subscription to either good girl or bad girl femininity. Many of the middle-class girls were quick to label themselves and each other as bad girls upon introduction of the day's topic, whereas, most of the girls from lower- and working-class backgrounds seemed reluctant to identify completely with either one.

Overall, the good girl persona did appear fairly important to most of the girls, especially the minority girls. They responded as follows:

> Researcher: So what girls care about being good girls?
> Molly: Me!
> Aaliyah: Me!
> Keisha: They wanna be good girls.
> Molly: I want to be
> Keisha: I would too.
> Salena: I don't.
> Keisha: You don't wanna be normal?
> Salena: I'm just messed up in the head today...

Therefore, according to the minority girls, being "good" was equated with being "normal," and they aspired to live up to this standard. The lower-status, working-class girls seemed to place a fair bit of emphasis on the standard of niceness upheld in the good girl persona arguing, "If you want to make more friends you have to be nice," "'Cause then you can keep all your friends and get more ones," "It is important [to be nice] because if you want like good results in how people treat you and all that, be nice, but if you want bad results just get all mean," "And if you aren't nice, then people will think you're really bad," "If you're bad, you won't get what you want… being a girl, you can get anything you want by beating your eyelashes" (she demonstrates) and "Sometimes you can end up down below… you know, with the devil if you're really bad sometimes." Certainly, these findings contradict the finding of Taylor, Gilligan and Sullivan (1995), Lamb (2001) and Simmons (2002) that middle-class girls endorse the good girl model of femininity more than working-class and/or minority girls. However, these findings are consistent with Laidler and Hunt's (2001) and Ness's (2004) findings that respectability is important to girls regardless of ethnic or cultural backgrounds, but middle-class girls have a variety of resources for expressing their femininity. This could also be the case for higher-status girls, as respectability was assessed largely on appearance and sexuality, while the lower-status girls viewed respectability as passivity and niceness.

Girl Fights

The girls identified different forms of girlfighting, for example, word or talking fights, with girls engaging in verbal confrontations and "burning contests," where girls would try to one up each other with insults. A "catfight," according to the girls, usually involves word fights and sometimes physical confrontations, such as pulling hair and pushing. However, some of the girls argued that catfights are not the same as a physical fight. For example, while the girls felt that popular girls fight most often, this was not viewed as physical fighting but, rather, as a catfight. The girls described a catfight in the following ways: "arguing," "talking fights," "They just push and talk," "They just talk back and give attitude," "I don't think they like punch, I think they just like push," "I think they catfight, like backtalk," "Like accidentally, they'll bump them and then they're like 'oops, sorry'" and "They get into these big catfights, usually at first they're just like saying bad words and stuff to each other and then they, they lose it, then they start punching and stuff, and then they're like 'oh my God, you just like broke my nail!'" In other words, catfights can involve physical confrontation, but they tend not to defy feminine boundaries too much in that they rarely involve traditionally masculine versions of violence, such as punching. These findings are consistent with Laidler and

Hunt (2001) and Ness's (2004) argument that girls who engage in physical fighting will often negotiate their femininity in line with their aggression.

Word Sanctions

In these, word fights, girls use words such as "bitch," "whore" and "slut." When asked what "slut" means, one girl defined it as "boyfriend taker, you're like flirting with someone you know that your friend likes or someone else likes and you dress like in mini-skirts and stuff to get their attention." This suggests that, as opposed to labels that typify a person, these words are used as sanctions or punishments. Word fights appeared highly significant to most of the girls as a talking fight gave a girl the opportunity to defend her reputation. One girl explains, "Usually when you back down from not a real fight but like a word fight... they make fun of you." Thus, winning a word fight is important to girls if they wish to maintain a certain amount of respect among their peers. The girls claimed that most talking fights usually occurred among popular girls but they could sometimes involve a popular girl and an unpopular girl. While the girls claimed that gossip and rumours often lead to girl fights, they also said that most fights between girls revolve around boys and jealousy. Citing reasons why they thought popular girls engage in more word fights, the girls said, "Most popular girls don't have as much to do maybe" and "Most popular girls, it's like all the teachers like them and stuff 'cause they have respect towards the teachers but they don't towards like outside teachers and adults." This suggests popular girls' meanness is tolerated more than that of other girls because of their higher-status.

Fighting the Feminine Way

Not all girls use words to resolve their conflicts; as one girl argues, "Some girls are powerful with words and [others are] powerful with physical stuff." Other girls were thought to engage in physical confrontations "because that's the only way they have to defend themselves if they're not good at comebacks" or "People say mean things to them and they go 'oh I don't have anything to say back so I'll punch you in the face.'" Over the duration of the sessions with the girls, there was one particular incident of a catfight that was discussed. It involved two higher-status, white girls from one of my focus groups. One of these girls explained the situation:

> Well... first of all Lindsay was hogging up the bathroom. She was loading on the lipstick, had her hair brush, she was just sitting in there. Melissa, you know Melissa spazzes when she doesn't get her way, she's like a six year old, so I didn't want Melissa spazzin because she had to go to the bathroom, and they were right strict that day, about one person in the

bathroom. So I said "Lindsay, get on out," and she's like "I'm busy," but she was in there loading on lipstick all around her lips, she was missing them entirely, and thought she was fine [laughter], and so I said "Melissa you might as well go in, and I'll take the blame," so Melissa went in, and Lindsay stomped out. Couple minutes later I was minding my own business, talking to Elizabeth and she comes over and ah, and she says to me, "you think you're all that" and I said, "I'm not the one loading on lipstick in the bathroom, bragging about my boyfriend who probably stole the ring he owns from his mother... and then we went on from there, and then she picked up the tape and I said "are you going to get your big, fat, ugly boyfriend after me and slap me with the tape?" She got up and see this on the side of my face? [points to bruise on cheek] that's from her hitting me in the face with tape! So I got in a fight and I jammed her in the stomach and pulled her hair. I admit it, I did it! Because she's a bitch! She's done stuff like that ever since the first day I've known her, she's a bitch, I'm sorry that's the truth about Lindsay!

Girls from another group also briefly mentioned this incident, saying: "Melanie and Lindsay, they fought yesterday, they were fist fighting," "Yeah 'cause Melanie seen Lindsay with Tyler," "'Cause Laura threw a roll of tape at Melanie," and "Lindsay was calling Melanie names, 'cause they both think they're popular, but they're not!"

Clearly, this suggests that, for these girls, competition over a boy, jealousy and maintaining a perceived popular status were reasons for this fight. The girls also suggested that this was acceptable behaviour because the fight mostly involved name-calling and according to the girls, the physical part of the conflict was relatively minor. It seems that even when physical fighting is involved, girls manage to do it in a way that can be rationalized and does not jeopardize their feminine status.

When asked whether girls who fight are any less girlie, the majority of the girls indicated that fighting does not necessarily make a girl less feminine. In fact, one girl said that, "No, I fight... oh and on WWE [World Wrestling Entertainment], you can have a bra and panty match. They have this fight in their bras and panties." The girls seemed to suggest that there are ways in which girls can use their sexuality in fights and maintain their femininity. This supports Currie and Kelly's (2006) research finding that girls behave in ways that will appeal to the male gaze.

Conclusion

Important themes pertaining to race and class arose in the girls' discussions. First, the girls indicated that most girls, independent of race and class, tend to hide their anger, especially from boys. However, the girls did claim that higher-status girls are able to target their anger towards other girls in the form of meanness. Recognizing that it is not acceptable to express their anger outwardly, the girls cited numerous ways in which they could get angry without becoming physically or directly aggressive. The girls also indicated that it was never completely acceptable for girls to use violence or aggression. However, it appeared that there are extenuating circumstances when it is warranted for girls to use aggressive force. The minority girls seemed more accepting of these particular situations as they reported that they had been taught by their parents to use aggressive force when necessary. On the other hand, most of the white girls indicated that they had been taught to avoid aggressive behaviour. The girls' perceptions of girls' aggression were notably racialized in that the girls viewed Black girls as more aggressive than white girls, attributing conditions of poverty and racial oppression as the reason for this difference.

In response to questions concerning race and class, the girls' responses indicated that both class and racial status are significant factors in determining how girls perceive aggression. More specifically, it seemed as though the lower-status girls were more accepting of girls' use of aggressive force in certain situations, such as for self-defence. On the contrary, the white, higher-status girls were somewhat forgiving of girls' aggression depending on the circumstance, while the white, lower-status girls were even less tolerant. All the white girls in my study claimed that they had been taught that it was inappropriate for girls to engage in violence or aggressive force. Overall, girls' lessons in aggression seemed to differ significantly along race and status categories. In addition, it also appeared that girls' perceptions and attitudes towards aggression influenced how they themselves expressed their aggression.

The final series of themes revolved around femininity. The higher-status girls seemed to participate in the evaluation of other girls' femininity more readily than the lower-status girls, who tended to turn the judgments onto themselves. It appeared that feminine appearance was an important measure of a girl's worth and even power among all the girls. For girls, being pretty can also be the necessary precursor to obtaining a higher level of power, that which is allocated through male admirers. However, according to the girls, standards of feminine beauty are heavily constrained by structures of class and especially race. This would indicate that power is more accessible to white, higher-status girls.

In relation to feminine personas, the girls were divided in their subscription to either good girl or bad girl femininity. Higher-status girls seemed to have more flexibility to perform both types of femininity, while lower-status girls attempted to maintain feminine performances that did not cast too far from good girl femininity, perhaps because they are more vulnerable to other girls' feminine evaluations. The girls identified catfights, word fights and talking fights as different types of girl fighting that conform to the rules of femininity. In other words, these types of girl fights largely consist of verbal confrontations, a reflection of the girls' perception of female power through words, not actions. According to the girls' narratives surrounding girl fights, even when girls do use physical aggression it is relatively minimal.

While the minority girls attested to the importance of being a good girl, they also indicated that they would use aggression when necessary. It seems that girls' feminine performances are carefully negotiated in line with their aggression to avoid male rejection and jeopardize their chances of gaining worth and power by becoming the object of male desire. The girls also indicated that girls' aggression is reflective of their feminine ideals. In other words, girls have adopted alternate ways in which to engage in confrontations that do not defy feminine standards. Thus, girls' feminization of aggression through meanness, as well as catfights and word or talking fights, does not challenge the privileging of male aggression. These forms of aggression all represent passive means of girls' negotiation of power. Finally, as indicated by the girls, feminine performances as well as girls' negotiations of femininity are reflective of their status position, which is ultimately constrained by structures of class and race.

Conclusion

Implications of Girl Talk

A persistent theme throughout this research is the extent to which the girls' understandings of concepts such as aggression, popularity, power, race, class and femininity differed from that of adults. On the whole, this raises serious epistemological concerns about our knowledge of girl culture and, thus, it has important implications for what aspects of girls' lives are problematized and the effectiveness with which these issues are then addressed.

A Motive for Meanness

Much of the research on relational aggression treats meanness as a state of being. More disconcerting is that relational aggression and meanness are often viewed as the result of mental disorders rather than a function of power relations. Consistent with the work of Owens, Shute and Slee (2000) and Crain, Finch and Foster (2005), the girls supported the notion that meanness is related to popularity. According to the girls, mean behaviour is more than just a descriptive feature of the popular girl profile: meanness is a mechanism whereby girls can negotiate their power and status among other girls. This finding is significant in supporting previous work by Merten (1997), Lease, Kennedy and Axelrod (2002), Phillips (2003) and Cillessen and Mayeux (2004) that linked meanness and social power.

One important association, which is not overly emphasized in the literature but was prevalent in my research, is the link between popularity and power. While the importance of popularity among girls is often downplayed and even mocked by adults, popularity represents one of the only avenues to power for girls. The girls' narratives surrounding the prominence of meanness suggest that this instrument of power negotiation is not solely reserved for popular girls. In particular, the girls indicated that attractiveness, whiteness and wealth are rewarded with popularity in girl culture. Thus, girls' access to power is fundamentally limited and heavily weighted on standards of femininity as well as structures of class and race. With few positions available at the top, girls learn to negotiate their status carefully through such mechanisms as gossip, meanness, catfights and word fights. All of these mechanisms endorse passive competition among girls for power and male approval without challenging the privileged status of male aggression and dominance.

Negotiating Power in Girl World

The girls' constant evaluation of each other's feminine appearance and performances suggests that femininity is girls' primary means of capital, as is also suggested by Proweller (1998), Best (2000), Bettie (2003), Harris (2004), Currie and Kelly (2006) and Jiwani (2006). The minority girls claimed that they would use aggressive force when necessary. Taylor, Gilligan and Sullivan (1995), Miller and White (2004), Chesney-Lind and Pasko (2004), Batacharya (2004) and Jiwani (2006) also suggested that girls' lessons in aggression are not always consistent across racial and class categories. Yet, femininity appeared to be central in the girls' discussions of girl aggression. It appeared that girls negotiate their feminine performances to ensure that they do not jeopardize their feminine reputations and more specifically, their opportunity to appeal to male admirers. This is not to say that race and class structures are not significant to the analysis of girl aggression. On the contrary, these findings suggest that it is important to examine how structures of race and class manifest themselves in the production of feminine hierarchies and, in turn, influence how girls negotiate their status and power among other girls.

Popularity was perceived by these girls as the primary determinant of social power among girls, and they indicated that being pretty was one of the most powerful qualities that a girl could possess. Yet, the girls' narratives surrounding beauty suggest that feminine standards are also racialized, with whiteness being perceived as the desirable model of femininity. Arguably, pretty, rich white girls have the greatest chance of exercising power because they fit the mold of ideal femininity. Thus, these findings illustrate the ways in which "hegemonic femininity" (Batacharya 2004) and structures of dominance (Jiwani 2006) are manifested in girl culture.

For those girls outside the realm of popularity and, presumably, white middle-class standards, power can sometimes be calculated in terms of niceness. As indicated by some of the lower-status girls, niceness was viewed as a means of gaining a likeable status among peers. Certainly, this finding is particularly important in that it challenges the work of Laidler and Hunt (2001), who argued that working-class girls might not be rewarded for their niceness to the same extent as middle-class girls. In addition, the girls' preoccupation with boyfriends indicates that male attention can also provide girls with a modicum of power. As well, these girls' power was also related to their consumption patterns, as suggested by Harris (2004). Finally, the girls showed some resentment about being girls and hopeful anticipation about becoming women as they felt there was more value and autonomy in becoming mothers than remaining girls. While the girls indicated that niceness, boyfriends, consumer consumption and eventual womanhood represent avenues to power and status, these are also related to structures of femininity.

Consequently, the feminine body is the site upon which girls' status, power and class is negotiated and awarded.

An analysis of the girls' perceptions of power further illustrates the constraints placed on girls and their ability to negotiate power. The girls perceived men's power in actions, while women's power was related to words. Thus, girls' engagement in aggression is conditioned by their gendered experiences of power; girls' power must be displayed in a passive-aggressive manner. Therefore, possessing power means a girl must learn to walk a thin line between extremes of femininity. For instance, a girl cannot be too skinny, too heavy, too smart, too aggressive, too nice or too sexual. Girls must learn to carefully negotiate their power and status in a way that is unthreatening to patriarchal structures and a society that celebrates male aggression. The girls' narratives surrounding social injustices, such as sexual and physical harassment by boys and men, adults' abuse of authority and racial discrimination, further exemplify the extent to which girls are constantly reminded of their state of powerlessness as both youth and girls. Consequently, the girls suggested that meanness is a mechanism whereby popular girls can maintain a higher status over their female peers, but this is not to say that only popular girls utilize meanness in their negotiations of status and peer hierarchies. Lower-status girls indicated that meanness is common among most girls but seems to be more apparent and even accepted among popular girls. Hence, meanness serves as a mechanism that allows all girls to combat feelings of powerlessness. Yet, for most girls, meanness is used in moderation to ensure that they do not jeopardize their only capital, femininity.

The Feminine Body in Class Construction

Obtaining status in girl culture is not necessarily about traditional class categories that locate individuals in specific income brackets; rather, status is more a reflection of femininity. As far as social class is concerned, these girls did not exclusively identify with their parent's socio-economic status. Instead, the girls' class-consciousness was largely determined by their feminine performances. Reay (2003), Bettie (2003), Ali (2003), Walkerdine (2003) and Lucey, Melody and Walkerdine (2003) also maintain that class is produced within the personal, cultural, sexual and social realms as well as the labour market. In particular, much of the girls' assessments of worth were weighted on the presentation of the feminine body, through fashion, hairstyle, skin care and dieting, thereby illustrating the dynamics of a "gendered economy" (Currie and Kelly 2006). Much of girls' power and status is located in feminine standards of attractiveness, as argued by Best (2000). Any of the girls who maintained a reasonably high status among peers seemed to do so because they possessed the material goods that made them feminine, attractive and, most importantly, sexually appealing to boys.

Without the ideal feminine appearance, it would seem that girls must rely on a secondary measure of the feminine body, the niceness clause. If a girl is not pretty she must at least be nice. Consequently, those girls who possess the desired feminine look (thin body, long, smooth and in most cases blonde hair, and name-brand clothing) seemed to hold the highest status among their peers and appeared more risqué in their feminine performances. More specifically, these girls frequently used curse words, appeared more forward with boys, openly discussed such topics as sex and occasionally dressed provocatively. The girls' working-class backgrounds seemed to have little bearing on the girls' status among their peers. In other words, maintaining a higher-status was primarily based on feminine appearance.

The girls who appeared to be in constant judgment of themselves for their acne, their dark complexion, their weight, their thick, curly hair and their "hand-me-down" clothing seemed to hold a lower status relative to other girls; however, they also seemed to pride themselves more on being nice, respectable girls. For the lower-status girls, being nice was equated with having multiple and long-lasting friendships and maintaining a "likeable" status among their peers. Presumably, the higher-status girls are not under the same pressure to appear nice or respectable as they possess the ultimate capital, enabling them to evaluate the femininity of other girls to secure their upper position. Due to their appropriate feminine appearance, it was not always necessary for them to prove their respectability as this is merely secondary to having a pretty face. Other girls must either conform to the "nice girl" persona or risk social rejection for rebelling against feminine standards. By locating girls' value exclusively in feminine standards, it would seem that a girl's socio-economic background does not automatically determine her status in girlhood; rather, femininity is the status marker in girl world. My findings suggest that the feminine hierarchy is played out, first and foremost, through appearance and secondarily through performance.

While Walkerdine (2003) and Lawler (2005) argue that respectability is central to working-class girls' class assignment, my findings suggest that generating a respectable persona is important to any girl who does not measure up to popular culture's idealized image of the feminine body, independent of her class category. Perhaps the discourse surrounding respectability is better suited to an analysis of women and class as, arguably, women have alternate means of capital, through their participation in the labour market. In this case, the class category of "working-class" seems to hold more consequence. To obtain respectability, lower-status girls may perform what is perceived to be a middle-class identity, where being nice, kind and polite is perceived as normal. The lower-status girls in this study subscribed to "good girl" femininity more readily than the higher-status girls. Thus, it would seem that girls' only capital appears to be their femininity and feminine standards, both of which provide more appropriate predictors of a girl's status than her parents' socio-economic background.

Race, Femininity and Aggression

Racial hierarchies seemed to play an important role both in girls' ability to perform white standards of femininity and in how the girls' perceptions of other girls' aggression differed. These findings are consistent with the work of Mirza (1992), Reay, (2001), Ali, (2003) and Bettie, (2003). The minority girls appeared more apt to subscribe to "good girl" femininity, presumably instilled by white, middle-class society, than most of the white girls from middle-class backgrounds. However, it would be difficult to conclude with any certainty that minority girls, or white girls for that matter, do or do not subscribe to a particular type of femininity. Indeed, Ali (2003) argues that it is problematic to assume that particular kinds of femininity can be intrinsically linked with particular kinds of racial or ethnic backgrounds. Yet, this finding makes a significant contribution to the research because it raises a major contradiction with the literature that suggests minority girls exhibit resistance toward white, middle-class standards of femininity that promote niceness (Taylor et al. 1995; Chesney-Lind and Shelden 1998; Lamb 2001; Simmons 2002 and Brown 2003). The literature implies that only white, middle-class girls bear the burden of such standards. My findings challenge these claims, suggesting that feminine standards can permeate race categories.

Despite their investment in "good girl" feminine performances, the minority girls also seemed more apt to forgo their nice demeanor in situations that warranted aggressive behaviour. For instance, these girls indicated that they had been taught by their families to use physical force when necessary, whereas, the white, middle-class and working-class girls indicated that they had been taught to suppress their aggression (Lamb 2001; Simmons 2002). This suggests that minority girls must negotiate their feminine performances in line with their aggression, as race structures can sometimes generate contradictory expectations of girls.

The girls identified specific racial stereotypes in relation to girls' aggression in that they perceived Black girls as more aggressive and assertive than white girls. This may indicate that girls are aware of the social standards that Lamb (2001), Simmons (2002) and Brown (2003) argue permit aggression among minority girls. However, it also exemplifies the hegemonic nature of femininity as the girls' perceptions of Black girls as more aggressive emphasize racial hierarchies in the production of feminine standards. These perceptions normalize the behaviour of white girls as incapable of doing wrong and reinforce the structures of "white" dominance. Furthermore, the girls indicated that many Black girls use aggression as a means of survival in conditions of poverty as well as to combat racial oppression. This further illustrates the dynamics of hegemonic femininity and the normalization of white privilege. The minority girls conceptualized this aggression in terms of "protecting their own" and they claimed that they would use aggressive force to stand up for a sibling or friend. Thus, they understood their aggression in terms of loyalty rather than oppression and power. This finding also suggests that "class" is racialized in relation to girls' aggression to the extent that being white is associated with privilege and being Black is associated with poverty and, in turn, violence.

While the minority girls did not seem to suppress aggression to the same extent as white girls, their testaments to the importance of niceness suggest that they are not completely adverse to performances of white, middle-class femininity. This contradicts the claims of Taylor, Gilligan and Sullivan (1995), Chesney-Lind and Shelden (1998), Lamb (2001), and Simmons (2002) that minority girls are not influenced by these standards of femininity.

Playing by the Rules of Femininity

The girls' narratives surrounding girlfighting indicated that girls strategically align their aggression with feminine standards. In other words, girls' status and power can be negotiated through passive aggressive tactics such as meanness as long as girls meet specific feminine requirements, namely, looking pretty or acting nice. In the face of suppressive genderization of girls' aggression, girls have developed alternate ways of engaging in more overt forms of aggressive behaviour without accumulating social stigma. Catfights or word and talking fights seem to be acceptable in girl world since passive acts of aggression, shoving, yelling, name-calling and even throwing objects conform to patriarchal and feminine standards. Thus, while Campbell (1993), Crowley Jack (1999), Simmons (2002) and Brown (2003) argue that girls are taught to avoid aggression, these findings illustrate that this is not always the case.

Language appears to be the central component within girl fights. Arguably, girls seek power by verbally demeaning another girl's femininity in a word or talking fight, where they will use such word sanctions as "slut" and "whore" to punish a girl for behaving in a sexualized manner. Hence, in the context of girlhood, where male attention gives power, flirting with another girl's boyfriend is perceived as a serious threat to that girl's status. Although adults commonly trivialize competition among girls for boys' interest, this competition is extremely important as it represents one of the only avenues to power that girls possess. To the extent that femininity is girls' only capital, sexuality is the target of criticism within these competitions. At the same time, some girl fights actually play on performances of sexuality, such as the

WWE matches, where women fight in their bra and panties. This type of girl fight is considered acceptable mainstream entertainment and it undoubtedly appeals to the sexual fantasies of men.

The girls' perception of male power also provides a context to girls' use of passive forms of aggression. In other words, the girls perceived men's power in terms of physical force, as also suggested by Artz (1998), and they perceived women's power in words. Evidently, girls comply with these gender norms, challenging other girls' status but never undermining the gender hierarchy. Girls must learn to negotiate their power carefully, in a way that is unthreatening to patriarchal structures. Girls' power can only be displayed in a passive-aggressive manner, and possessing power means a girl must learn how to walk a thin line between extremes. For instance, a girl cannot be too skinny, too heavy, too smart, too aggressive or too sexual. Arguably, pretty, rich white girls have the greatest chance of experiencing power because they fit the feminine standards that attract men as well as the resources to affectively negotiate their position in the gendered economy.

Conclusion

While my sample was small and by no means representative of all girls, this does not detract from the important theoretical, methodological and epistemological contributions of my findings. Theoretically, my research provided a framework of analysis that goes beyond the problematization of girls' meanness and examined the ways in which structures of femininity and race shape girls' lives. While I had initially embarked on an examination of class and girl aggression, the results of my research indicate that class is not necessarily the central issue and suggest that girls' aggression should be framed within the context of feminine hierarchies in future research. Whether it is meanness, relational aggression or even girl bullying, these labels distract from the underlying issues at hand. The problem is not mean girls or even violent girls; rather, these adult-defined phenomena are produced and reproduced through hierarchies of dominance. Research on girl aggression needs to account for the ways in which hierarchical structures of race and gender are built into structures of femininity.

Another theoretical contribution of my research comes from its expansion of previous discourses on femininity. First, although Merten (1997), Lease, Kennedy and Axelrod (2002), Phillips (2003) and Rose, Swenson and Walker (2004) found a connection between popularity, power and meanness, they did not examine how structures of femininity affect this relationship. My findings suggest that popularity represents power, which is constrained by feminine hierarchies. In addition, while structures of femininity in the context of class formation are highlighted in the work of Walkerdine (2003),

Hey (2003), Reay (2003) and Lawler (2005), their discussions concentrate primarily on working-class women and respectability. My research suggests that adult class categories do not hold as much meaning in girl culture as the hierarchies of dominance manifested through structures of race and femininity.

I frequently noted discrepancies between the girls' experiences and adult-produced discourse and research in the conceptualizations of concepts such as meanness, popularity, race, class and femininity throughout the focus group discussions. Using adult definitions in studying girls is both methodologically and epistemologically problematic. While adults posing as "experts," such as James Garbarino, continue producing and influencing popular discourse on girls' aggression, it is questionable whether such versions of girls' behaviour accurately reflect girls' realities. Where meanness has been problematized by researchers as relational aggression and by school officials and parents as bullying, in the context of girl culture, meanness is a resilient strategy employed by girls to negotiate power and status.

The privileging of adults' knowledge over that of girls has major epistemological consequences. My research has illuminated some of the ways in which our knowledge of girls' aggression is flawed. In talking to girls and positioning them as the "experts," I uncovered important gaps in what we think we know about girl culture. More importantly, these discrepancies between adults' and girls' knowledge of girl aggression have implications for what is being problematized and how it is being addressed. Overall, this research exemplifies the need for a theoretical and practical deconstruction of the hierarchies of dominance that structure girls' lives. Liberation from these constraints will only occur with an appreciation of girls' knowledge and a willingness to learn from their experiences.

References

Abbott, P., and R. Sapsford. 1987. *Women and Social Class*. London: Tavistock Publications.

Acker, J. 1973. "Women and Social Stratification: A Case of Intellectual Sexism." *American Journal of Sociology* 78.

Alder C., and A. Worrall. 2004. "A Contemporary Crisis?" In C. Alder and A. Worrall (eds.), *Girls' Violence: Myths and Realities*. Albany: State University of New York Press.

Ali, S. 2003. "To be a Girl: Culture and Class in Schools." *Gender and Education* 15, 3.

Armstrong, P., H. Armstrong, and A. Miles. 1985. *Feminist Marxism or Marxist Feminism: A Debate*. Toronto: Garamond Press.

Artz, S. 1998. *Sex, Power and the Violent School Girl*. Toronto: Trifolium Books.

_____. 2004. "Violence in the Schoolyard: School Girls' Use of Violence." In C. Alder and A. Worrall (eds.), *Girls' Violence: Myths and Realities*. Albany: State University of New York Press.

Barron, C. 2000. *Giving Youth a Voice: A Basis for Rethinking Adolescent Violence*. Halifax: Fernwood Publishing.

Barron, C., and D. Lacombe. 2005. "Moral Panic and the Nasty Girl." Canadian Review of Sociology and Anthropology/Revue Canadienne de Sociologie et d'anthropologie 42, 1.

Barton, B.K., and R. Cohen. 2004. "Classroom Gender Composition and Children's Peer Relations." *Child Study Journal* 34, 1.

Batacharya, S. 2004. "Racism, 'Girl Violence,' and the Murder of Reena Virk." In C. Alder and A. Worrall (eds.), *Girls' Violence: Myths and Realities*. Albany: State University of New York Press

Batchelor, S.A., M.J. Burman, and J.A. Brown. 2001. "Discussing Violence: Let's Hear it for the Girls." *Probation Journal* 48, 2.

Bell, S. 2006. *Young Offenders and Youth Justice: A Century After the Fact (3rd ed.)*. Canada: Nelson.

Best, A.L. 2000. *Prom Night: Youth, Schools, and Popular Culture*. New York: Routledge.

Bettie, J. 2003. *Women without Class: Girls, Race, and Identity*. Los Angeles: University of California Press.

Bierman, K.L., C. Bruschi, C. Domitrovich, G.Yan Fang, S. Miller-Johnson and the Conduct Problems Prevention Research Group. 2004. "Early Disruptive Behaviors Associated with Emerging Antisocial Behavior among Girls." In M. Putallaz and K.L. Bierman (eds.), *Aggression, Antisocial Behavior, and Violence among Girls*. New York: Guilford Press.

Björkqvist, K., K.M.J. Lagerspetz and A. Kaukiainen. 1992. "Do Girls Manipulate and Boys Fight? Developmental Trends in Regard to Direct and Indirect Aggression." *Aggressive Behavior* 18.

Björkqvist, K., and P. Niemelä. 1992. "New Trends in the Study of Female Aggression." In K. Björkqvist (ed.), *Of Mice and Women: Aspects of Female Aggression*. San Diego: Academic Press.

Brendgen, M., G. Dionne, A. Girard and M. Boivin. 2005. "Examining Genetic and Environmental Effects on Social Aggression: A Study of Six-Year-Old Twins." *Child Development* 76, 4.

Bright, R.M. 2005. "It's Just a Grade 8 Thing: Aggression in Teenage Girls." *Gender and Education* 17, 1.

Brinson, S. 2005. "Boys Don't Tell on Sugar-and-Spice-but-not-so-Nice Girl Bullies." *Reclaiming Children and Youth* 14, 3.

Brown, D.K. 2001. "Lack of Girls' Comics Reduces Role Models." *Independent* 3, June.

Brown, M.L. 2001. "Voicing Silence and Anger in Girls' Relationships with Other Girls." Available at <http://www.colby.edu/personal/l/lmbrown/article2.doc> (accessed November 17, 2003).

Brown, L.M. 2003. *Girlfighting: Betrayal and Rejection Among Girls.* New York: New York University Press.

Burman, M. 2004. "A View from the Girls: Challenging Conceptions of Violence." *Sociology Review* 13, 4.

_____. 2004. "Turbulent Talk: Girls' Making Sense of Violence." In C. Alder and A. Worrall, (eds.), *Girls' Violence: Myths and Realities.* Albany: State University of New York Press.

Burstyn, V., and D. Smith. 1985. *Women, Class, Family and the State.* Toronto: Garamond Press.

Buss, A. 1961. *The Psychology of Aggression.* New York: Wiley.

Camodeca, M., F.A. Goossens, M. Meerum, and C. Schuengel. 2002. "Bullying and Victimization Among School-age Children: Stability and Links to Proactive and Reactive Aggression." *Social Development* 11, 3.

Campbell, A. 1984. *The Girls in the Gang.* New York: Basil Blackwell.

_____. 1990. "Female Participation in Gangs." In R.C. Huff (ed.), *Gangs in America.* Newbury Park: Sage.

_____. 1993. *Men, Women, and Aggression.* New York: Harper Collins.

Carlo, G., M. Raffaelli, D.J. Laible and K.A. Meyer. 1999. "Why are Girls Less Physically Aggressive than Boys? Personality and Parenting Mediators of Physical Aggression." *Sex Roles: A Journal of Research.* May.

Casey-Cannon, S., C. Hayward and K. Gowen. 2001. "Middle-School Girls' Reports of Peer Victimizations: Concerns, Consequences, and Implications." *Professional School Counselling* 5, 2.

Chesney-Lind, M., and M. Brown. 1999. "Girls and Violence." In D. J. Flannery and C. R. Huff (eds.), *Youth Violence: Prevention, Intervention, and Social Policy.* Washington: American Psychiatric Press.

Chesney-Lind, M., and K. Irwin. 2004. "From Badness to Meanness: Popular Constructions of Contemporary Girlhood." In A. Harris (ed.), *All About the Girl: Culture, Power, and Identity.* New York: Routledge.

Chesney-Lind, M., and L. Pasko. 2004. *The Female Offender: Girls, Women, and Crime (2nd ed.).* California: Sage Publications.

_____. (eds.). 2004. *Girls, Women, and Crime: Selected Readings.* California: Sage Publications.

Chesney-Lind, M., and R.G. Shelden. 1998. *Girls: Delinquency and Juvenile Justice (2nd ed.).* California: Wadsworth Publishing.

Cillessen, A.H., and L. Mayeux. 2004. "From Censure to Reinforcement: Developmental Changes in the Association Between Aggression and Social Status." *Child Development* 75, 1.

Conway, A.M. 2005. "Girls, Aggression, and Emotion Regulation." *American Journal of Orthopsychiatry* 75, 2.

Crain, M.M., C.L. Finch and S.L. Foster. 2005. "The Relevance of the Social Information Processing Model for Understanding Relational Aggression in Girls." *Merril-Palmer Quarterly* 51, 2.

Crick, N.R., and J.K. Grotpeter. 1995. "Relational Aggression, Gender and Social-Psychological Adjustment." *Child Development* 66.

Crothers, L.M., J.E. Field and J.B. Kolbert. 2005. "Navigating Power, Control, and Being Nice: Aggression in Adolescent Girls' Friendships." *Journal of Counseling & Development* 83.

Crowley, Jack D. 1999. *Behind the Mask: Destruction and Creativity in Women's Aggression.* Cambridge: Harvard University Press.

Cummings, A.L., and A.W. Leschied. 2000. "Understanding Aggression with Adolescent Girls: Implications for Policy and Practice." *Canadian Journal of Community Mental Health* 20, 2. Available at <http://www.crvawc.ca/docs/pub_cummings2001.pdf> (accessed November 17, 2003).

Currie, D.H. 1999. *Girl Talk: Adolescent Magazines and Their Readers.* Toronto: University of Toronto Press.

Currie, D.H., and D.M. Kelly. 2006. "'I'm Going to Crush You Like a Bug': Understanding Girls' Agency and Empowerment." In Y. Jiwani, C. Steenbergen, and C. Mitchell (eds.), *All About the Girl: Culture, Power and Identity.* New York: Routledge.

Davis, Y.A. 1983. *Women, Race and Class.* New York: Random House.

Devault, M.L. 1996. "Talking Back to Sociology: Distinctive Contributions of Feminist Methodology." *Annual Review of Sociology* 22.

Dhruvarajan, V., and J. Vickers. 2002. *Gender, Race and Nation: A Global Perspective.* Toronto: University of Toronto Press.

Driscoll, C. 1999. "Girl Culture, Revenge and Global Capitalism: Cybergirls, Riot Grrls, Spice Girls." *Australian Feminist Studies* 14, 29.

Dyer, R. 1988. "White." *Screen* 29.

Eckert, P. 1989. *Jocks and Burnouts: Social Categories and Identity in High School.* New York: Teachers College Press.

Ehrenreich, B. 1976. "What is Socialist Feminism?" *Monthly Review* July–August.

_____. 1989. *Fear of Falling: The Inner Life of Middle Class.* New York: Monthly Review Press.

_____. 2005. "What is Socialist Feminism?" *Monthly Review* 70–77.

Ellen, B. 2000. "8 Going on 18." *Life Magazine* December 3.

Fine, M. 1997. "Sexuality, Schooling, and Adolescent Females: the Missing Discourse of Desire." In M. Gergen and S. Davis (eds.), *Toward a New Psychology of Gender.* New York: Routledge.

Flannery, D., and C.R. Huff (eds.). 1999. *Youth Violence: Prevention, Intervention, and Social Policy.* Washington: American Psychiatric Press.

Giles, J.W. 2005. "Young Children's Beliefs about the Relationship between Gender and Aggressive Behavior." *Child Development* 76, 1.

Gilligan, C. 1990. "Teaching Shakespeare's Sister: Notes from the Underground of Female Adolescence." In C. Gilligan, N.P. Lyons and T.J. Hanmer (eds.), *Making Connections: The Relational Worlds of Adolescent Girls at Emma Willard School.* Massachusetts: Harvard University Press.

_____. 1993. "Joining the Resistance: Psychology, Politics, Girls and Women." In L. Weis and M. Fine (eds.), *Beyond Silenced Voices: Class, Race and Gender in United States Schools.* Albany: State University of New York Press.

Gilligan, C., and L.M. Brown. 1992. *Meeting at the Crossroads: Women's Psychology and Girls' Development.* Cambridge, MS: Harvard University Press.

Goodwin, M.H. 2002. "Exclusion in Girls' Peer Groups: Ethnographic Analysis of Language Practices on the Playground." *Human Development* 45.

Graydon, S. 1999. "Bad Girls." *Homemakers Magazine,* March. Available at <http://www.reseau-medias.ca/english/resources/articles/stereotyping/bad_girls.cfm> (accessed December 10, 2004).

Griffin, C. 2004. "Good Girls, Bad Girls: Anglocentrism and Diversity in the Constitution of Contemporary Girlhood." In A. Harris (ed.), *All About the Girl: Culture, Power and Identity.* New York: Routledge.

Grotpeter, J.K., and N.R. Grotpeter. 1996. "Relational Aggression, Overt Aggression and Friendship." *Child Development* 67.

Harris, A. 2004. "Jamming Girl Culture: Young Women and Consumer Citizenship." In A. Harris (ed.), *All About the Girl: Culture, Power and Identity.* New York: Routledge.

Hey, V. 1997. *The Company She Keeps: An Ethnography of Girls' Friendships.* Buckingham: Open University Press.

_____. 2003. "Joining the Club? Academia and Working-class Femininities." *Gender and Education,* 3.

Hipwell, A.E., R. Loeber, M. Stouthamber-Loeber, K. Keenan, H.R. White and L. Kroneman. 2002. "Characteristics of Girls with Early Onset Disruptive and Antisocial Behaviour." *Criminal Behaviour and Mental Health* 12.

It's a Girl's World: A Documentary about Social Bullying. 2004. The National Film Board of Canada.

Jiwani, Y. 2006. *Discourses of Denial: Mediations of Race, Gender, and Violence.* Vancouver: UBC Press.

_____. 2006. "Racialized Violence and Girls and Young Women of Colour." In Y. Jiwani, C. Steenbergen and C. Mitchell. (eds.), *Girlhood: Redefining the Limits.* Montreal: Black Rose Books.

Joe, K., and M. Chesney-Lind. 1995. "'Just Every Mother's Angel': An Analysis of Gender and Ethnic Variations in Youth Gang Membership." *Gender and Society* 9.

Kehily, M.J. 2004. "Girls and Sexuality: Continuities and Change for Girls in School." In A. Harris (ed.), *All About the Girl.* New York: Routledge.

Laidler, K.J., and G. Hunt. 2001. "Accomplishing Femininity Among Girls in the Gang." *British Journal of Criminology* 41.

Lamb, S. 2001. *The Secret Lives of Girls: What Good Girls Really Do — Sex Play, Aggression, and Their Guilt.* New York: Free Press.

Lawler, S. 2005. "Disgusted Subjects: The Making of Middle-Class Identities." *The Sociological Review.*

Lease, A.M., C.A. Kennedy and J.L. Axelrod. 2002. "Children's Social Constructions of Popularity." *Social Development* 11, 1.

Leschied, A.W., A. Cummings, M. Van Brunschot, A. Cunningham and A. Saunders. 2000. *Female Adolescent Aggression: A Review of the Literature and the Correlates of Aggression.* Ottawa: Public Works and Government Services Canada.

Litosseliti, L. 2003. *Using Focus Groups in Research.* London: Continuum.

Loukas, A., S.K.Paulos and S. Robinson. 2005. "Early Adolescent Social and Overt Aggression: Examining the Roles of Social Anxiety and Maternal Psychological Control." *Journal of Youth and Adolescence* 34, 4.

Lucey, H., J. Melody and V. Walkerdine. 2003. "Uneasy Hybrids: Psychological Aspects of Becoming Educationally Successful for Working-class Young Women." *Gender and Education* 15, 3.

Maccoby, E.E., and C.N. Jacklin. 1974. *The Psychology of Sex Differences.* Stanford: Stanford University Press.

Messerschmidt, J.W. 1986. *Capitalism, Patriarchy and Crime: Towards a Socialist Feminist Criminology.* New Jersey: Rowman and Littlefield Publishers.

_____. 1997. *Crime as Structured Action: Gender, Race, Class and Crime in the Making.* Thousand Oaks: Sage.

McRobbie, A. 2000. *Feminism and Youth Culture.* New York: Routledge.

_____. 2004. "Feminism and the Socialist Tradition... Undone?" *Cultural Studies* 18, 4.

Mean Girls. 2004. Paramount Pictures.

Merton, D.E. 1997. "The Meaning of Meanness: Popularity, Competition, and Conflict among Junior High School Girls." *Sociology of Education* 70, 3.

Miller, J., and N.A. White. 2004. "Situational Effects of Gender Inequality on Girls' Participation in Violence." In C. Alder and A. Worrall (eds.), *Girls' Violence: Myths and Realities.* Albany: State University of New York Press.

Mirza, H. 1992. *Young, Female and Black.* London: Routledge.

Molidor, C.E. 1996. "Female Gang Members: A Profile of Aggression and Victimization." *Social Work* 41, 3.

Moretti, M.M., R. Holland and S. McKay. 2001. "Self-Other Representations and Relational and Overt Aggression in Adolescent Girls and Boys." *Behavioral Sciences and the Law* 19.

Ness, C.D. 2004. "Why Girls Fight: Female Youth Violence in the Inner City." *The Annals of the American Academy* 59.

Newman, K. 1989. *Falling from Grace: The Experience of Downward Mobility in the American Middle Class.* New York: Vintage Books.

Odd Girl Out. 2005. Maple Pictures.

Olweus, D. 1978. *Aggression in the Schools: Bullies and Whipping Boys.* Washington: Hemisphere Publishing Corp.

_____. 1993. *Bullying at School: What We Know and What We Can Do.* Oxford and Cambridge: Blackwell.

Orenstein, P. 1994. *Schoolgirls: Young Women, Self-Esteem, and the Confidence Gap.* New York: Doubleday.

Ortner, S. 1991. "Reading America: Preliminary Notes on Class and culture." In R. Fox (ed.), *Recapturing Anthropology: Working in the Present.* Santa Fe: School of American Research Press.

Ostrov, J.M., N.R. Crick and C.F. Keating. 2003. "Gender-biased Perceptions of Preschoolers' Behavior: How Much is Aggression and Prosocial Behavior in the Eye of the Beholder?" *Sex Roles* 52.

Owens, L., R. Shute and P. Slee. 2000. "I'm In and You're Out: Explanations for Teenage Girls' Indirect Aggression." *Psychology, Evolution and Gender* 2, 1.

Parker, J.G., C.M. Low, A.R. Walker and B.K. Gamm. 2005. "Friendship Jealousy in Young Adolescents: Individual Differences and Links to Sex, Self-Esteem, Aggression, and Social Adjustment." *Developmental Psychology* 41, 1.

Phillips, C. 2003. "Who's Who in the Pecking Order? Aggression and 'Normal Violence' in the Lives of Girls and Boys." *British Journal of Criminology* 43, 4.

Prinstein, M.J., J. Boergers and E.M. Vernberg. 2001. "Overt and Relational Aggression in Adolescents: Social-Psychological Adjustment of Aggressors and Victims." *Journal of Clinical Child Psychology* 30, 4.

Proweller, A. 1998. *Constructing Female Identities: Meaning Making in an Upper Middle Class Youth Culture.* Albany: State University of New York Press.

Putallaz, M., and K.L. Bierman (eds.). 2004. *Aggression, Antisocial Behavior, and Violence Among Girls: A Developmental Perspective.* New York: Guilford Press.

Putallaz, M., J.B. Kupersmidt, J.D. Coie, K. McKnight and C.L. Grimes. 2004. "A Behavioral Analysis of Girls' Aggression and Victimization." In M. Putallaz and K.L. Bierman (eds.), *Aggression, Antisocial Behavior, and Violence Among Girls: A Developmental Perspective.* New York: Guilford Press.

Reay, D. 1996. "Insider Perspectives or Stealing the Words out of Women's Mouths: Interpretation in the Research Process." *Feminist Review* 53.

_____. 2001. "'Spice Girls,' 'Nice Girls,' 'Girlies,' and 'Tomboys': Gender Discourses, Girls' Cultures and Femininities in the Primary Classroom." *Gender and Education* 13, 2.

_____. 2003. "A Risky Business? Mature Working-Class Women Students and Access to Higher Education." *Gender and Education* 15, 3.

Remillard, A.M., and S. Lamb. 2005. "Adolescent Girls' Coping with Relational Aggression." *Sex Roles* 53.

Riley, R. 2002. "Ignored by Parents, Girl Bullies Run Wild." *Detroit Free Press,* June 14.

Rosaldo, R. 1993. *Culture and Truth: The Remaking of Social Analysis.* Boston: Beacon Press.

Rose, A.J., L.P. Swenson and E.M. Walker. 2004. "Overt and Relational Aggression and Perceived Popularity: Developmental Differences in Concurrent and Prospective Relations." *Developmental Psychology* 40, 3.

Russell, A., and L. Owens. 1999. "Peer Estimates of School-Aged Boys' and Girls' Aggression to Same and Cross-Sex Targets." *Social Development* 8, 3.

Salmivalli, C., A. Kaukiaiken and K. Lagerspetz. 2000. "Aggression and Sociometric Status Among Peers: Do Gender and Type of Aggression Matter?" *Scandinavian Journal of Psychology* 41.

Save the Last Dance. 2001. Paramount Pictures.

Schissel, B. 1997. *Blaming Children: Youth Crime, Moral Panics and the Politics of Hate.* Halifax: Fernwood Publishing.

Simmons, R. 2002. *Odd Girl Out: The Hidden Culture of Aggression in Girls.* New York: Harcourt.

_____. 2004. *Odd Girl Speaks Out: Girls Write about Bullies, Cliques, Popularity, and Jealousy.* Orlando: Harcourt Publishing.

Skeggs, B. 1997. *Formations of Class and Gender.* London: Sage.

Smith, D. 1987. *The Everyday World as Problematic: A Feminist Sociology.* Toronto: University of Toronto Press.

Smith, H., and S.P. Thomas. 2000. "Violent and Nonviolent Girls: Contrasting Perceptions of Anger Experiences, School, and Relationships." *Issues in Mental Health Nursing* 21.

Stanley, L., and S. Wise. 1990. "Feminist Praxis: Method, Methodology and Epistemology in Feminist Sociology." In L. Stanley (ed.), *Research, Theory and Epistemology in Feminist Sociology.* London: Routledge.

Stermac, L. 1998. "Aggression and Girls." *MacLean's,* 11, 25.

Sumrall, S.G., G.E. Ray and P.S. Tidwell. 2000. "Evaluations of Relational Aggression as a Function of Relationship Type and Conflict Setting." *Aggressive Behavior* 26..

Susman, E.J., and K. Pajer. 2004. "Biology: Behavior Integration and Antisocial Behavior in Girls." In M. Putallaz and K.L. Bierman, (eds.), *Aggression, Antisocial Behavior, and Violence Among Girls: A Developmental Perspective.* New York: Guilford Press.

Talbot, M. 2002. "Girls Just Want to be Mean." *The New York Times Magazine,* February 24.

Talbott, E., D. Celinska, J. Simpson and M.G. Coe. 2002. "Somebody Else Making Somebody Else Fight: Aggression and the Social Context among Urban Adolescent Girls." *Exceptionality* 10, 3.

Taylor-McLean J., C. Gilligan and A.M. Sullivan. 1995. *Between Voice and Silence: Women and Girls, Race and Relationship.* Cambridge: Harvard University Press.

Tomada, G., and B.H. Schneider 1997. "Relational Aggression, Gender, and Peer Acceptance: Invariance across Culture, Stability over Time, and Concordance among Informants." *Developmental Psychology* 33, 4.

Underwood, M.K. 2003. *Social Aggression among Girls.* New York: Guilford Press.

Vail, K. 2002. "Relational Aggression in Girls." *American School Board Journal* 189.

Walkerdine, V. 2003. "Reclassifying Upward Mobility: Femininity and the Neo-Liberal Subject." *Gender and Education* 15, 3.

Walkerdine, V., H. Lucey and J. Melody. 2001. *Growing up Girl: Psychological Explorations of Gender and Class.* New York: New York University Press.

Werner, N.E., and N.R. Crick. 2004. "Maladaptive Peer Relationships and the Development of Relational and Physical Aggression during Middle Childhood." *Social Development* 12, 4.

Werner, N.E., and C.L. Nixon. 2005. "Normative Beliefs and Relational Aggression: An Investigation of the Cognitive Bases of Adolescent Aggressive Behavior." *Journal of Youth and Adolescence* 34, 3.

Zahn-Waxler, C, and N. Polanichka. 2004. "All Things Interpersonal: Socialization and Female Aggression." In M. Putallaz and K.L. Bierman (eds.), *Aggression, Antisocial Behavior, and Violence among Girls: A Developmental Perspective.* New York: Guilford Press.

Zalecki, C.A., and S.P. Hinshaw. 2004. "Overt and Relational Aggression in Girls with Attention Deficit Hyperactivity Disorder." *Journal of Clinical Child and*

Adolescent Psychology 33, 1.

Zoccolillo, M., D. Paquette, R. Azar, S. Côté and R. Tremblay. 2004. "Parenting as an Important Outcome of Conduct Disorder in Girls." In M. Putallaz and K.L. Bierman, (eds.), *Aggression, Antisocial Behavior, and Violence among Girls: A Developmental Perspective.* New York: Guilford Press.